MAKING Fabergé-style EGGS

MAKING
Fabergé-style
EGGS

DENISE HOPPER

GUILD OF MASTER CRAFTSMAN PUBLICATIONS

First published 2002 by
Guild of Master Craftsman Publications Ltd
Castle Place, 166 High Street,
Lewes, East Sussex BN7 1XU

Text and drawings © Denise Hopper 2002
© in the work GMC Publications 2002
Photographs by Anthony Bailey, © GMC Publications Ltd 2002
Photographs styled by Grant Bradford

ISBN 1 86108 296 7

A catalogue record for this book is available from the British Library.

Edited by Stephen Haynes
Book and cover designed by Christopher Halls at Mind's Eye Design, Lewes
Set in Goudy

Colour origination by Viscan Graphics (Singapore)
Printed in China by Sun Fung Offset Binding Co Ltd

CONTENTS

ACKNOWLEDGEMENTS

First of all, thanks to my Mum, Catherine, who first introduced me to this craft; also to my sons, who have had to fend for themselves on more than one occasion while this book was being written. Many thanks for the numerous cups of tea, boys! I would also like to mention the two Sarahs: Sarah Trencher for her unending support and encouragement, and Sarah Oakes for her help and support where the 'cursed machine' is concerned – in layman's terms, the computer.

The following have been particularly helpful in providing specialist products and information: June Eccles of Eggstravaganza, Saltwater House, Longlands Road, Middlesbrough, Cleveland TS4 2JR; Linda Martin of Linda Martin Egg Designs, 173 High Cross Road, Poulton-le-Fylde, Lancashire FY6 8BX.

INTRODUCTION

Since the dawn of time, eggs have symbolized fertility and rebirth; they have been decorated and given as gifts throughout the centuries in all kinds of different cultures. The eggs in this book have been inspired by the work of Carl Fabergé, jeweller to the Russian royal family in the late nineteenth and early twentieth centuries. Fabergé's eggs were fashioned from precious metals and gems, and are still collected today; the eggs in this book are made from real blown eggshells and decorated using braids, beads and Austrian crystals. Each egg is a work of art in itself.

You will not need any specialist tools to start you off with this hobby, and all the items you do need are easily bought by mail order from eggcrafting catalogues. It is a very rewarding hobby, and the finished items make perfect gifts for friends and family.

I hope that the eggs shown in this book will inspire you to go on and create new designs of your own.

Happy egging!

TOOLS
AND MATERIALS

To start with, you won't need any specialist tools or equipment: my first egg was marked using a wide elastic band, a sharp pencil and a tape measure, and I cut it with a craft knife. I have even read that if you soak the eggshell for long enough it is possible to cut it with scissors, though I must admit I have never been brave enough to try!

Always wear a protective face mask when sanding down and cutting the egg; it is also advisable to wear goggles whenever possible, especially when cutting the larger eggshells, as they tend to splinter.

As you become more accomplished you will undoubtedly want to try more intricate designs. This is when you will find an egg marker and a hobby drill or turbine drill invaluable.

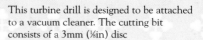

This turbine drill is designed to be attached to a vacuum cleaner. The cutting bit consists of a 3mm (⅛in) disc

An egg marker is a tool that makes marking and dividing the egg into sections much easier and more accurate. It has 12 sides, and comes in two different sizes. The smaller one is ideal for the very tiny eggs such as quail, up to large goose eggs; the larger size, which I use, can take from quail up to ostrich-sized eggs. Like everything else used in this book, they are available from most eggcraft suppliers' catalogues, which are advertised in craft magazines.

All the eggs used in this book have been bought pre-blown from eggcraft suppliers.

Almost any type of paint can be used, from sample pots of emulsion (latex paint) to good-quality acrylics, but always try to buy the best that you can afford. I use acrylic paints on most of my eggs, and the majority of the projects in this book were painted using Duncan's pearl and golden sheen, available from eggcraft suppliers, which give a beautiful finish.

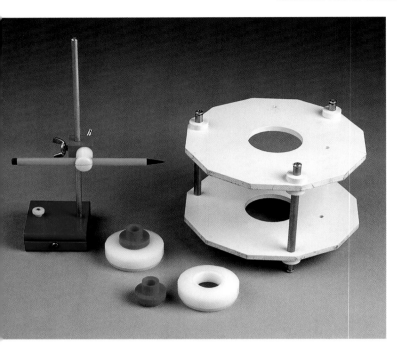

The Jem egg marker with its accessories. Other makes are available, and all come with instructions for use

A couple of good-quality paintbrushes are a must – you will never achieve a flawless finish with a cheap brush. I recommend an artist's no. 4 and no. 6 round, and a 6mm (¼in) chisel (flat) brush for varnishing; if taken care of, these will last for years.

There are two main types of glue used: a tacky glue, such as Velverette, for applying braids and beads and for lining the inside of the shell, and a two-part epoxy resin. The tubes of epoxy are easier to control than the syringe, especially when mixing small amounts. A cocktail stick is ideal for applying a thin line of tacky glue, and also for mixing the epoxy resin.

Fine-grade glasspaper is used to rub the egg down prior to marking, and wet-and-dry is used when 'sinking' a print.

Petroleum jelly (Vaseline) is used on the hinge posts to help prevent glue from getting into the post and seizing up the hinge.

Polyflakes are a kind of fine glitter which will give a beautiful lustre to a plain eggshell; a medium glitter is also available, as used on the inside of the Gothic-Style Egg on page 27. Both types come in many colours. Crystalina is similar to polyflakes, but is white, and available only in the fine size. Hairspray makes a good sealing agent to set polyflakes to the shell.

A selection of braids, beads and filigrees will be needed to decorate the shell, and figures to go inside the diorama-style eggs; you can build up a

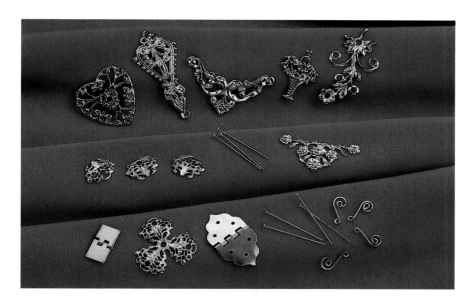

Fittings available from eggcraft suppliers include various hinges and a wide range of filigrees, some of which can be used as hinge covers. The larger hinges are attached with pins

collection of these in time. I can't walk past a charity shop these days without popping in to see what goodies they have – old pieces of costume jewellery, for instance, always come in useful, as do small ornaments.

Stands are available in various sizes from all the main eggcraft suppliers. Most of them can be had in gold or silver, and some ceramic stands are also available. Try painting the stands for added interest: first paint the chosen area with ordinary acrylic, and then go over this when it is dry with the pearl or golden sheen paints.

A selection of different materials, such as satin and velvet, will come in handy when lining the shell. As a general rule I use a medium-weight polyester satin, and on occasion velvet.

Micropore (surgical tape) is used to cover the blowhole from the inside of the egg, and then the hole is *overfilled* with a ready-mixed decorator's filler (such as Polyfilla) from the outside. When this is set, it is then rubbed down flush with the outer shell so you can't see where the hole was.

A small juice bottle, filled with small stones or sand to give it weight, makes a good aid when painting the shell.

A decorator's sponge with an egg-shaped hole pulled out of the middle will hold the egg when adding braids and beads. It is also a good idea to have a soft cloth or folded towel on your work surface, as this reduces the risk of the shell cracking if it should slip out of your hands.

A hairdryer can be used to speed drying between coats of paint – two or three thin coats are better than one thick coat. Always make sure that the paint is dry before recoating – damp or wet paint feels cold to the touch, so if it is cold leave it alone for a little longer.

CHAPTER 1

THE BASIC CUT

The basic cut described in this chapter is also used on many of the other projects in the book. It is a classic and versatile shape which lends itself to many different decorative styles.

A SIMPLE EGG

This attractive and straightforward design introduces many of the basic eggcraft techniques. I have described the processes in detail because once you have mastered them you can use them time and time again.

You will need the following items to make this simple egg:

- a tall goose egg
- fine-grade glasspaper
- tape measure
- egg marker or elastic band
- craft knife, or hobby drill and 3mm (⅛in) drill bit
- paints, brush and/or sponge
- epoxy resin and tacky glue (such as Velverette)
- small hinge and petroleum jelly (Vaseline)
- filigree suitable for use as a hinge cover
- a stand suitable for an upright goose egg
- a selection of braids and beads (I used fine gold cord and picot-edged braid)
- material for lining the inside of the shell.

Select an egg of suitable size and shape for your chosen project, and very gently rub down the eggshell with fine-grade finishing paper to remove any lumps and bumps from the surface of the shell. Take your time and rub down the whole of the shell; it should feel smooth and have a slight sheen to it before you start marking.

MARKING THE SHELL

Now that the egg has been rubbed down, you are ready to start marking. The method described here is suitable for beginners, as you won't need any specialist equipment.

Take a tape measure and measure around the egg from top to bottom and back up the other side; or you might find it easier to wrap a piece of wool or string around the egg and measure that instead. A quarter of this measurement gives you the position of the centre line of the egg. For example, if the egg measures 24cm all of the way around, then your halfway measurement is 6cm from the top (Fig 1.1). Place a light pencil mark at this point. (It makes no difference whether you measure in centimetres or inches; use whichever you prefer, but stick to one or the other – do not try to mix them.)

Now place the elastic band around the egg, slightly above this centre mark (Fig 1.2). Keep nudging the band until you are happy that it is straight, then with a sharp pencil mark in the cut line.

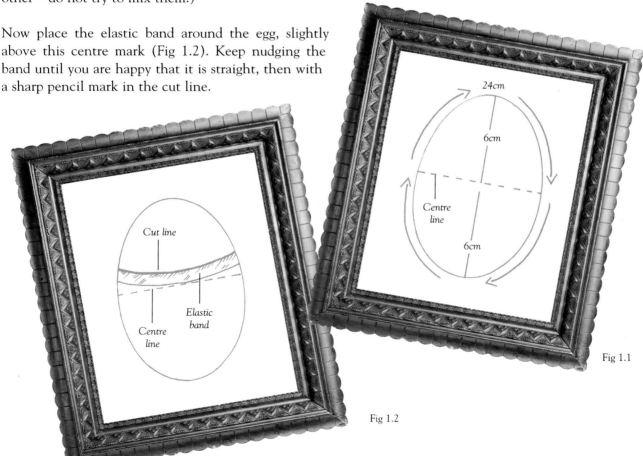

Fig 1.2

Fig 1.1

You are now ready to mark where the hinge will go. Remove the elastic band and make a small pencil mark on the cut line, then measure the width of the hinge. If the hinge measures 8mm, for example, you will place marks 4mm either side of your first small mark on the cut line (Fig 1.3).

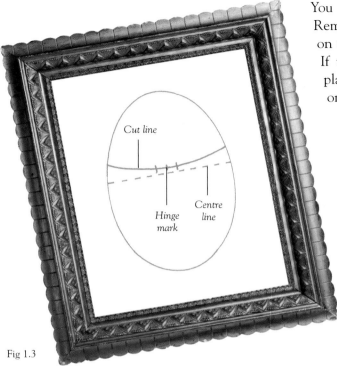

Fig 1.3

CUTTING THE EGG

Before starting to cut, remove any unnecessary pencil marks. The first egg I ever made was cut using a craft knife; this method is fine for basic eggs with straight edges. Gently score around the whole of the shell, keeping to the cut line, and going in one direction only. Scratch all of the way through the shell; never use a sawing motion, or the egg will likely break. Take your time, as this is quite a time-consuming method of cutting the shell. The shell will make a loud popping sound when it separates.

The easiest and one of the best ways to cut the egg is to use a hobby drill or a turbine drill. The turbine drill is my favourite; it is much like an air drill in that there is very little vibration, and is simple and easy to use, with a little practice. It is an ingenious invention: a hose and pneumatic rotor that fits onto a cylinder vacuum cleaner. Both types of drill and a selection of craft knives are available from most of the good mail-order egg catalogues.

When cutting the egg, never cut all of the way through in one go; instead, score small sections at a time and then cut through. By doing this you minimize the chance of a jagged break; if the egg does break, it is more likely to do so along the scored edge.

Once the egg has been cut open you will need to clean away the excess membrane from the inside. Hold the open piece of shell under a cold running tap for a few minutes, and gently peel away the membrane.

Leave the egg to dry for a few hours, and then fill in the blowhole. Cover the hole from the inside with Micropore and then use a ready-mixed decorator's filler (such as Polyfilla) to fill in the hole from the outside. Once dry, rub down with the finishing paper until you can't see where the hole was.

PAINTING THE SHELL

Before painting the shell, transfer your hinge marks to the inside of both base and lid sections so they will not be covered up.

The most important thing to remember when painting or varnishing the shell is that two or three thin coats are better than one thick coat. Don't overwork an area, and always leave plenty of drying time between coats. You can use a hairdryer to speed-dry between coats, but be careful you don't blow the egg halfway across the room!

You can either use a brush or a sponge to paint the egg. First of all, apply a thin base coat of matt acrylic paint (not the thicker 'gesso base', which is too lumpy) to seal the shell; this will also conceal any blemishes that couldn't be removed with the glasspaper. If you are planning a light-coloured finish, use a white or cream base paint; when using dark colours, try to keep your base coat as near as possible to the final colour. Leave to dry thoroughly before adding your final finish. I use Duncan's pearl and golden sheen on most of my eggs.

A coat or two of water-based varnish will strengthen and protect the shell. Suitable varnishes include Royal Coat, used in découpage and available from most craft outlets.

LINING THE SHELL

Drape the tape measure inside the egg from one side to the other and add 2cm (¾in); you can add more if you want a fuller lining. Using a compass, mark a circle of this diameter on your piece of material, and cut out. To make cutting easier and to avoid fraying, I coat my guideline with a thin line of tacky glue.

Stitch close to the edge of the material, using a running stitch. Gather the material so it will fit to the inside of the egg; it is important that you don't gather it too small, or it won't fit the shell.

Place a line of tacky glue on the inside of the egg, close to the edge (it is easiest to use an old paintbrush to apply the glue), and place the lining inside, sticking the sewn edge to the glue. Add a piece of braid to cover the sewn edge of the lining, but don't go too close to the cut edge of the shell or the egg won't close properly.

Repeat for the lid, adjusting the measurements accordingly.

HINGING THE EGG

There are several different ways to set the hinge onto the shell; this first method is particularly suitable for eggs cut with a craft knife.

Before painting, you cleaned the membrane from the inside of the shell and transferred the hinge marks to the inside. After it has been painted, transfer these marks back to the outside of the shell, lining them up so that they match top and bottom, and place a few pieces of low-tack masking tape or Micropore over the join to secure the top to the bottom.

You will have to bend the hinge slightly so it sits neatly and securely against the curved surface of the egg; do this gently, using pointed pliers. Score the hinge with a craft knife or other sharp object where it will meet the shell, and gently scratch the shell where the hinge will sit; this is to give a key for the glue to adhere to (Fig 1.4).

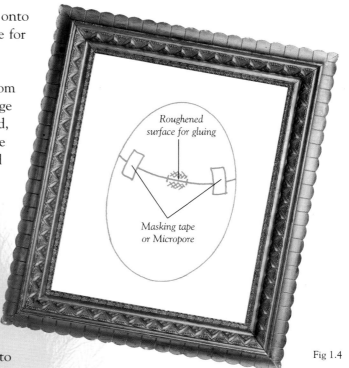

Fig 1.4

Put plenty of Vaseline (petroleum jelly) over the hinge post. This is to prevent glue from getting into the post and seizing up the hinge; it is very important that you do this to every hinge.

Mix equal amounts of epoxy resin and hardener, and place a small amount onto the egg where the hinge will sit, but not too close to the cut edge. Carefully place the hinge onto the egg and gently press it into the glue, making sure that the hinge post is straight and in line with the cut edge of the shell (Fig 1.5). Leave to set.

Glue a decorative filigree over the hinge. If it needs trimming, this can be done with a pair of wire cutters. Don't place the edge of the filigree against the post of the hinge, or it will stop the lid opening properly.

Fig 1.5

ADDING DECORATION

Using either a cocktail stick or a small glue bottle, apply a thin line of tacky glue close to the cut edge of the egg. Press on a row of the fine gold cord, keeping it straight. When this is set, add a row of beads, followed by a row of the picot-edged braid. Repeat for the top, but leaving out the beads.

FINISHING

Choose a suitable stand for the size of the egg. Lightly scratch the bottom of the egg and the cup part of the stand with a piece of glasspaper.

Mix equal amounts of epoxy resin and hardener, put some epoxy resin into the cup of the stand, and with the egg at eye level (you will probably have to kneel on the floor) place the egg into the cup. As the glue begins to set, rotate the stand to make sure that the egg is straight from all angles; if you place a ruler on the table in an upright position next to the egg, as shown in the photograph below, it is easier to see if it is straight by using the beads as a guide.

The other two eggs in this chapter are both cut, painted and lined in the same way as the first, but they look quite different because of the final decoration. The last one has more marking than the other two, and this is made easier with an egg marker, but it is still possible to do it using a tape measure.

FILIGREE EGG

This project introduces a further element of decoration in the form of ready-made filigrees, which can be bought from eggcraft or jewellery catalogues. A wide range is available; choose them carefully to suit the size and shape of the egg you are using.

For this next project you will need:

- a tall goose egg
- fine-grade glasspaper
- craft knife, or hobby drill and 3mm (⅛in) drill bit
- egg marker or elastic band
- paints, brush and/or sponge
- epoxy resin and tacky glue
- small hinge and petroleum jelly
- a stand suitable for an upright goose egg
- fine gold cord
- 8 filigrees
- material for lining the inside of the shell.

Prepare the egg following the instructions given for the previous project, up to 'Adding decoration'.

When the egg has been painted, lined and hinged, you will need to add the filigrees and gold cord.

Place a row of gold cord at the cut edge of both the top and bottom parts of the egg. Gently bend each of the filigrees so they will fit neatly onto the shell, and glue them into position using small amounts of epoxy resin.

Glue the egg to the stand as before and, if you wish, attach a finial to the top in the same way.

STRINGS OF PEARLS

The shell of this egg is divided into narrow vertical panels to give an enamel-like effect. Careful marking out is essential.

For this project you will need:

- a tall goose egg
- fine-grade glasspaper
- craft knife, or hobby drill and 3mm (⅛in) drill bit
- egg marker or elastic band
- paints, brush and/or sponge
- epoxy resin and tacky glue
- small hinge and petroleum jelly
- filigree suitable for a hinge cover
- a stand suitable for an upright goose egg
- a selection of braids
- pearl chain or strung beads
- material for lining the inside of the shell.

After rubbing down the egg you will need to find the centre points at top and bottom (this is not necessary if you are using an egg marker). To do this, place the egg on its end onto a piece of carbon paper and turn it so the carbon leaves a spot on the shell. Do this for the top and the bottom of the egg.

Find the centre of the egg's height as before, and then divide the circumference into six sections, placing the hinge marks in the middle of one of these sections (Fig 1.6). Mark in your cut line.

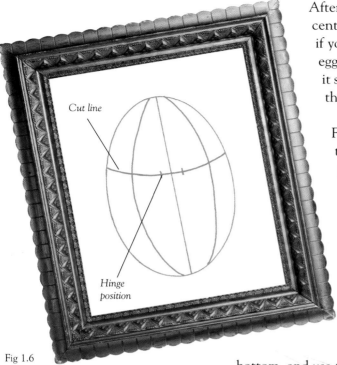

Cut line

Hinge position

Fig 1.6

The easiest way to divide the egg is to use an egg marker. If you haven't got one, then measure around the egg at the cut line with a tape measure and divide this measurement into the required number of equal parts. To draw in the vertical lines without an egg marker, use a rubber band as described for the first project (page 9). Place it around the egg from top to bottom, and use the pencil marks as a guide to line the band up all the way around the egg. Keep nudging it until it is straight, as before; repeat this until all the vertical lines have been drawn in.

Cut and clean the egg, fill the blowhole and rub down to a flush finish when dry. Paint the outside of the shell, redefining your guidelines between coats; it is important that you can see the lines when you add the decoration to the shell. If you are using a hobby drill to cut this egg, you could score in the horizontal guideline before cutting the egg open. When the paint is dry, attach the hinge as before and leave to set.

Fix the egg to its stand before adding the final decoration.

Using your marked lines as a guide, glue lengths of the pearl chain (for a less expensive alternative you could use strung beads), then add the fine gold cord to each side of the chain.

CHAPTER
2

THE SCALLOPED CUT

This technique adds a new dimension to your work, the curve of the scallops complementing the overall shape of the egg. You can make the lid and base interlock, or combine a scalloped edge with a straight edge to produce a series of windows onto the inside.

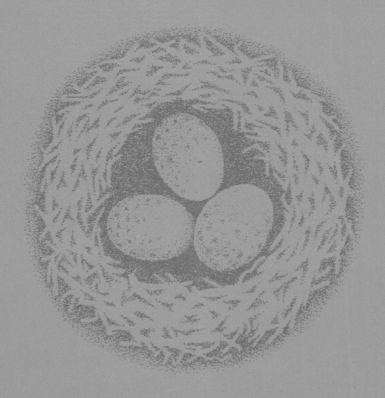

A CLASSIC SCALLOPED LID

I tend to do six scallops on most of my scalloped eggs, but they can look just as nice with three or four. I also prefer to have a straight edge on the base, mainly because it is easier to line a straight edge than a scalloped one. This style of egg is almost impossible to cut using a craft knife, so instructions will be given for using a drill.

For this project you will need:

- a tall goose egg
- fine-grade glasspaper
- egg marker or elastic band
- hobby drill and 3mm (⅛in) drill bit
- paints, brush and/or sponge
- water-based varnish
- epoxy resin and tacky glue
- small hinge and petroleum jelly
- a filigree suitable for use as a hinge cover
- a stand suitable for an upright goose egg
- a selection of braids and beads
- base for the egg
- 6 pearl hearts
- pastel ultrafine polyflakes
- material for lining the inside of the shell.

Prepare the egg by rubbing down to a smooth sheen.

Divide the egg into 12 sections (using the method described on page 18 if you don't have an egg marker), mark in the cut line and the hinge marks as before. Depending on how deep you want the scallops to be, mark in a further two lines above the cut line (Fig 2.1).

Using the vertical and horizontal lines as a guide, draw in the scallops so that each scallop covers two boxes, making allowances at the back for the width of the hinge (Fig 2.2).

When making this type of egg, I always attach the hinge before cutting the egg open completely, as this ensures that the lid is on straight. Remember to remove any unnecessary pencil marks before you start to cut the egg.

Mark in where the hinge post will be and cut this small section out; keep testing that the hinge will sit on the egg snugly with the post inwards. Cut either side of the opening for the hinge post, then attach the hinge to the egg, placing the post to the inside. Remember to add plenty of petroleum jelly to the post before gluing into position. Leave to set.

To cut the egg open, first cut out the scalloped edge, trying to keep the top edge of the drill towards the scallop, as this will give a cleaner, smoother curve to the cut. Once you have cut all of the way around the egg, you can then cut out the small pieces of shell to give a straight edge to the bottom half of the egg. Remember to score first: when doing the scalloped edge it is best to score all of the way around before cutting, as this will minimize the risk of the egg breaking. Both scoring and cutting are done with the drill; I would not attempt to do this type of cut using a knife.

The small photograph on the next page shows the scallops being cut with the turbine drill; you can see that the lines have already been scored.

If the membrane in the lid of the egg is clean and intact, don't remove it; just clean and remove the membrane from the bottom, and tidy up the edges on the lid with finishing paper.

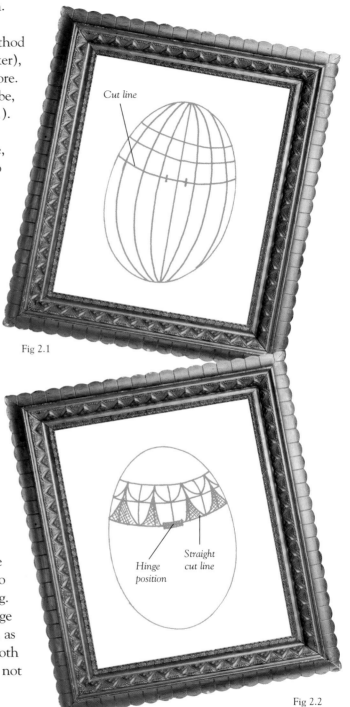

Cut line

Fig 2.1

Hinge position

Straight cut line

Fig 2.2

Paint the inside of the lid first, and when it is dry give it a coat of varnish and sprinkle on the ultrafine polyflakes. Once the varnish is dry you can seal the polyflakes with hairspray.

Paint the outside of the shell and line the bottom part. When the paint is dry, add the fine gold cord to the scalloped edge. Carefully paint the lower section in the contrasting colour; once dry, varnish and add the polyflakes in the same way as you did inside the lid, sealing with hairspray.

Using the photograph as a guide, decorate the outer shell and attach the finished egg to the stand.

If you are going to set the stand onto a base as I have done, decorate this in the same way as the egg, and then with some well-mixed epoxy resin set the stand onto the base. Leave to set.

GOTHIC-STYLE EGG

This is an example of an interlocking joint between lid and base. The shallow ogee (S-shaped) curves give this design something of a Gothic Revival flavour.

You will need the following items for this egg:

- a tall goose egg
- fine-grade glasspaper
- egg marker or elastic band
- hobby drill and 3mm (⅛in) drill bit
- paints, brush and/or sponge
- water-based varnish
- epoxy resin and tacky glue
- small hinge and petroleum jelly
- filigree suitable for use as a hinge cover
- a stand suitable for an upright goose egg
- picot-edged braid
- fine gold cord
- crystal chain or strung beads
- peel-off transfer
- medium polyflakes
- material to make a cushion to go inside the egg.

Prepare the eggshell and remove any blemishes.

Divide the egg into 12 sections. Mark in the cut line and two equally spaced lines above the cut line; don't make these too deep, as the scallops on this egg are quite shallow.

Fig 2.3

Mark in the hinge position, including the small cut-out for the hinge post, and then, using your pencilled boxes as a guide, draw in the S-shaped scallops (Fig 2.3), remembering to adjust the shape of one of them, as before, to make allowance for the hinge. Fit the hinge before cutting the egg open; once it is set, score all of the scalloped edges and then cut open.

Once the egg has been cleaned and all unnecessary pencil marks removed, paint the inside of the shell, both lid and base, making sure it has a good covering of paint. Leave to dry, then paint the outside of the shell also.

Carefully peel off the transfer from the backing paper and attach to the egg; you may have to trim it to fit onto the curve of the shell. Give the outside of the shell at least three coats of varnish, allowing plenty of drying time between coats.

Varnish the inside of the lid and sprinkle on the polyflakes; repeat for the bottom. Once dry, seal with hairspray.

Make a small cushion from a contrasting material to sit in the bottom of the egg. Cut out a circle of the material (I used organza and gold mesh), and sew all round close to the cut edge. Gather the whole thing in so it is tight, then sew the middle together. Add a small amount of tacky glue to the inside of the shell and gently press the cushion into position.

Trim the inside edges of the shell with the picot-edged braid, and do the edges of the lid in the same way. For the base, first trim with the fine gold cord, followed by the crystal chain and more gold cord, and finally the picot-edged braid.

Attach the egg to the stand.

SCALLOPS AND SWAGS

In this design the draped chain provides a foil or counterpoint to the scalloped edge, greatly adding to the richness of the effect.

You will need the following:

- a tall goose egg
- fine-grade glasspaper
- egg marker or elastic band
- hobby drill and 3mm (⅛in) drill bit
- paints, brush and/or sponge
- water-based varnish
- epoxy resin and tacky glue
- small hinge and petroleum jelly
- filigree suitable for use as a hinge cover
- a stand suitable for an upright goose egg
- picot-edged braid
- crystal chain
- 6 small roses
- 6 small bows
- Crystalina
- material to line the base.

Prepare the shell, mark in the cut line, hinge position and scallops as before, cut out the section for the hinge post and attach the hinge.

Cut the egg open, clean the inside and paint in your chosen colour, using a contrasting colour for the inside of the lid. Coat with the Crystalina and seal with hairspray.

Line the base of the egg, finishing off the edge with braid.

Decorate the scallops with the picot-edged braid, and then add the crystal chain so that it drapes evenly over the gap; finally, add the roses and bows, and the hinge covers.

Glue the egg to the stand.

USING TRANSFERS

The addition of transfers to a plain shell can have a remarkable effect. The following three eggs all use the styles of cut already described, but just look at the difference between the Basic Egg and the Jewelled Egg: the initial cut is the same but the finished result is totally different. I love the floral and cherub styles of transfers, but there are numerous other styles on the market, from wildlife to religious subjects. There are some beautiful Christmas ones, and phrases like 'Happy Birthday' or 'Congratulations' are also available to really personalize the finished egg.

GLITTERING
FLORAL EGG

In this design, floral transfers and sparkling polyflakes are combined with a variant of the scallop cut to give a rich but uncluttered effect.

You will need the following:

- a tall goose egg
- fine-grade glasspaper
- egg marker or elastic band
- hobby drill and 3mm (⅛in) drill bit
- paints, brush and/or sponge
- water-based varnish (I used Royal Coat)
- epoxy resin and tacky glue
- small hinge and petroleum jelly
- filigree suitable for use as a hinge cover
- small waterslide transfers
- polyflakes – golden tint
- crystal chain or strung beads
- choice of braids
- a stand suitable for an upright goose egg
- material to line the egg.

Prepare the shell in the usual way, making sure you have a good glossy finish before marking.

Mark your cut line slightly above the centre, and then place another mark about 1cm (⅜in) above your first line. Divide the egg into 12 sections, and mark in wavy scallops (Fig 3.1). Mark the hinge position and make the cut-out for the hinge post, as before. Attach the hinge, remembering to add the Vaseline to the post first; when set, cut the egg open.

Fill the blowhole with filler; when set, rub down to a flush finish with the egg.

Base-coat the outer shell with acrylic paint and leave to dry. Paint the lid of the egg white, and the base a golden colour; I used Duncan's 'white mist' on the top and 'gold lamé' on the bottom of my egg. Once the paint is thoroughly dry, coat the base with varnish, and while this is still wet sprinkle over the polyflakes (I used 'golden tint'). Leave to dry, then seal with hairspray.

Fig 3.1

Apply the waterslide transfers to the lid of the egg. The easiest way is to soak the transfer in a bowl of lukewarm water for a few seconds, then remove it from the backing paper and position it on the eggshell. Smooth into place, removing any air bubbles and creases; if you keep it quite wet, it is easier to adjust. Seal with a hairdryer set at warm. Be careful not to stretch the transfer out of shape as it warms up with the heat of the dryer. Give the lid several coats of varnish and leave to dry.

You can either line the inside of the egg with satin, or paint it and then add polyflakes, in which case you should make a small cushion (as described on page 26) to finish off the base.

Attach fine gold cord to the outer cut edges of the egg, followed by the crystal chain, gold braid, and then picot-edged braid for the base.

Glue the egg onto the stand.

JEWELLED EGG

This egg makes a lovely birthday gift. I made this one for my sister, whose birthstone is amethyst; just change the colour of the crystal to whatever birthstone you want.

You will need the following:

- a tall goose egg
- fine-grade glasspaper
- egg marker or elastic band
- craft knife, or hobby drill and 3mm (⅛in) drill bit
- paints, brush and/or sponge
- water-based varnish
- epoxy resin and tacky glue
- small hinge and petroleum jelly
- filigree suitable for use as a hinge cover
- small waterslide transfers
- choice of braids
- approximately 15 packets (depending on the size of your egg) of 3mm (⅛in) flat-backed crystals
- a stand suitable for an upright goose egg
- material to line the egg.

Prepare, mark, cut and hinge the egg in the same way as for the basic egg. Alternatively, you could attach the hinge before cutting the egg open.

Base-coat with acrylic paint. When dry, paint the lid white and the base a suitable colour to tone with the crystals; I have chosen lilac to go with the amethyst. Paint a little way inside the lid and base of the shell.

Line the inside of the egg using the circular method described in Chapter 1, and trim with a contrasting braid.

Apply the transfers to the lid of the egg; I have used nine small violet transfers to complement the amethyst crystals. Once you have done all the transfers, seal them with the hairdryer and several coats of varnish.

Add the gold braid to the outer cut edges of the shell; I have chosen to use a wide braid as this gives a richer look to the finished egg.

Working from the top of the base and using tacky glue, add the crystals row by row. Don't place them so that one crystal touches the next, but leave small gaps between them so the next row down will sit evenly. (You may have to change the spacing towards the bottom.) You will not need to carry them right to the bottom of the base, which will be covered by the stand. Once you have put on enough crystals to cover the lower part of the shell, glue the egg to the stand. I added some crystals to the stand to pull everything together.

A CASKET-CUT EGG

This egg was quite round, which is an ideal shape for a 'casket' cut. The egg lies on its side and the wide lid opens like an oyster shell.

You will need the following:

- a round goose egg
- fine-grade glasspaper and wet-and-dry paper
- egg marker or elastic band
- hobby drill and 3mm (⅛in) drill bit
- paints, brush and/or sponge
- water-based varnish
- Diamond Shimmer
- epoxy resin and tacky glue
- small hinge and petroleum jelly
- filigree suitable for use as a hinge cover
- waterslide transfer
- choice of braids
- up-eye, chain and beads to make a handle
- a stand suitable for a casket goose egg
- material to line the base.

Prepare the eggshell in the usual way.

Place the egg in the marker and turn onto its side. Mark in the centre line front and back. Now move the pencil up the rod of the scribe about 5mm (about ¼in) and then, using the knob on the bottom of the scribe, tilt the pencil until it touches the egg and mark in the lines front and back again. Turn the egg marker up the correct way and add the centre marks, then remove the egg from the marker and place small pencil marks at the top and bottom points of the egg. All these marks are guides for adding the scalloped edge to the egg. Allowing for the hinge, mark in the scallops (Fig 3.2).

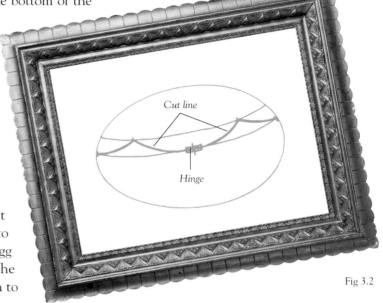

Fig 3.2

Place the hinge mark slightly off-centre, cut out for the hinge pin and glue the hinge into position as before. When set, cut the egg open, clean the inside of the shell and fill the blowhole. When the filler has set, rub down to a flush finish with the egg.

Paint the outer shell and the inside of the lid, and apply two coats of Diamond Shimmer (a type of varnish which goes on white but dries clear and glittery) to the inside of the lid.

Add the transfer to the lid of the egg, seal with the hairdryer and add two or three coats of varnish; rub down with wet-and-dry paper and give a further three coats, drying thoroughly after each coat. Again rub down with wet-and-dry, then give a final coat of varnish. You should not be able to see the edge of the transfer.

Fig 3.3

I used a different method of lining for the base of this egg. First, measure around the egg and add 1cm (⅜in). Next, measure the depth of the inside of the egg and add 3cm (1¼in); you need the extra material to allow for the scalloped edge. Cut a piece of material to these measurements, make a small hem at one end (Fig 3.3) and then form the material into a tube, using tacky glue.

Wrong side

Gathered edge

Fig 3.4

Use small stitches to gather one end (Fig 3.4). Now apply tacky glue to the inside of the base close to the cut edge, and, placing the gathered edge in the centre of the base, gently press the material into the glue. When dry, trim away the excess material. Edge with braid, and add matching braid to the inside of the lid.

Add your chosen braids to the outer shell, and a small handle to open the egg. The chain handle is secured to the door by an up-eye – a flat plate, glued to the egg surface, with a loop fixed to it to take the chain.

Glue the finished egg to the stand.

CHAPTER 4

THE
QUEEN ANNE CUT

This elegant variation is not as difficult as it looks. We shall cover a conventional and a reversed Queen Anne cut in this chapter. I don't normally do a full lining on this type of egg, due to the awkward shape of the cut edge, but for the purpose of this book I will line two and give instructions.

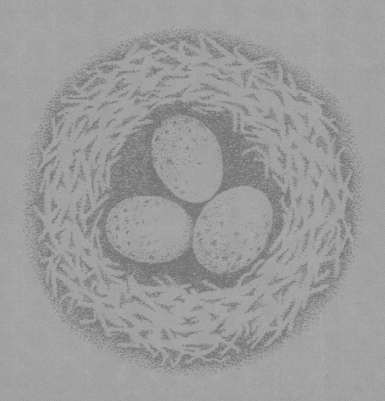

MARBLED EGG

The understated finish makes the Queen Anne shape itself the main focus of this graceful design.

You will need the following:

- a tall goose egg
- fine-grade glasspaper
- egg marker or elastic band
- hobby drill and 3mm (⅛in) drill bit
- paints, brush and/or sponge
- water-based varnish
- epoxy resin and tacky glue
- small hinge and petroleum jelly
- filigree suitable for use as a hinge cover
- floral crystal chain
- a stand suitable for an upright goose egg
- material to line the inside of the egg.

First prepare the eggshell in the usual way, making sure you have a good base to start with. Place the egg into the marker and turn onto its side to mark in centre lines front and back. Turn upright and mark in a straight cut line as usual. Remove the egg from the marker and, depending on how deep you want the V to be, place a light pencil mark below the cut line. Using the vertical line as a guide, now measure equal distances to either side of the centre point and draw in the V by eye (Fig 4.1).

The hinge marks must be placed directly behind the V, using the vertical centre line at the back as a guide.

Cut out the section for the hinge post as described on page 23 and attach the hinge. Now cut the egg open, being careful not to break the point off the V. Clean the inside, removing any excess membrane, fill the blowhole and, when dry, rub down to a flush finish.

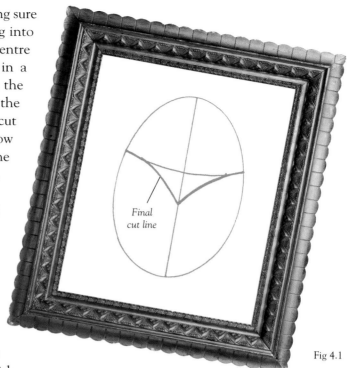

Fig 4.1

Paint the outer shell in your chosen colour. I gave mine a base coat of white and then marbled over that with 'golden pink' and 'purple iris' by Duncan's. To achieve this effect, let the base coat dry, then apply small dabs of the pink and purple, using a small sponge or a brush, letting them mix on the shell. You can apply the paint quite thickly to give a 'hammered' effect to the finished egg, but this will take about two days to dry thoroughly before adding the trimmings.

To line the inside of the lid, you need to mark out the circle of material as usual, and then add a point to it to allow for the extra piece of shell on the lid (Fig 4.2). For the base, mark out your circle of material and make a curved V towards the centre. Using small stitches, gather the material and glue in place. Add braid to the outer edge, but don't go too close to the cut edge of the shell or the egg won't close properly.

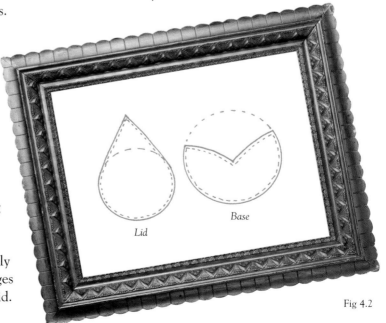

Fig 4.2

I have kept this egg very simple, and the only outer decoration is gold braid at the cut edges and one row of floral crystal chain on the lid.

Finally, glue the egg to the stand.

REVERSED QUEEN ANNE CUT

The same cutting technique, but with the V pointing upwards, gives a rather regal, tiara-like effect.

You will need the following:

- a tall goose egg
- fine-grade glasspaper
- egg marker or elastic band
- hobby drill and 3mm (⅛in) drill bit
- paints, brush and/or sponge
- Diamond Shimmer
- epoxy resin and tacky glue
- small hinge and petroleum jelly
- filigree suitable for use as a hinge cover
- a selection of braids and beads
- a stand suitable for an upright goose egg
- material to line the inside of the egg.

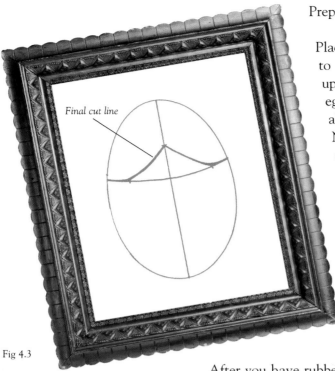

Final cut line

Fig 4.3

Prepare the eggshell in the usual way.

Place the egg into the marker and turn it onto its side to mark in centre lines front and back, then turn it upright and mark in a straight cut line. Remove the egg from the marker and place a light pencil mark above the cut line, using the vertical line as a guide. Now measure equal distances on either side of the centre point and draw in the upside-down V by eye, curving the mark so it sits well with the lower cut line (Fig 4.3).

Making sure the hinge marks are directly behind the upside-down V (use the vertical centre line as a guide), cut out the space for the hinge pin and glue the hinge into position. When set, cut the egg open, taking extra care at the pointed section, clean the inside of the shell and fill the blowhole as usual.

After you have rubbed down the filler in the blowhole, paint the egg in your chosen colour. When you are satisfied with the paint finish and all of the paint is dry, give the outer shell one or two coats of the Diamond Shimmer and leave to dry. The Diamond Shimmer looks white at first, but will dry clear, and gives a nice sparkle to the finished egg.

Line the egg in the same way as for the previous design, but reversing the layout for lid and base accordingly. Alternatively, you could make a small platform from a circle of card to fit into the bottom; paint it to match the egg, then glue it in with tacky glue. Finish the inside of lid and base with coats of water-based varnish and polyflakes.

Decorate the outer shell with your chosen braids and beads.

Glue the egg to the stand.

OSTRICH-EGG CASKET

The large size of this egg gives scope for a particularly opulent treatment, using a number of the techniques covered in earlier chapters.

You will need the following:

- an ostrich egg
- fine-grade glasspaper
- egg marker or elastic band
- hobby drill and bits suitable for cutting an ostrich egg
- paints, brush and/or sponge
- waterslide transfer
- ultrafine polyflakes
- water-based varnish
- hairspray
- epoxy resin and tacky glue
- large hinge (with holes) and six pins
- filigree suitable for use as a hinge cover
- petroleum jelly
- fine gold cord
- crystal and pearl chain, or strung beads, to match the paint colour
- wide braid
- bow filigree
- a stand suitable for an ostrich egg
- material to line the inside of the egg.

Don't be put off working with the larger eggs; these eggs are lovely to work with and are harder to break because the shells are so much thicker. They are also a little bit more difficult to cut, and the ostrich egg especially tends to splinter when cutting. I would advise anyone cutting any egg to wear goggles and a mask, but especially when cutting the larger eggshells.

Rub the outer shell down to remove any blemishes, but don't overdo it as you don't want to loose the natural effect of the shell.

Place the egg into the marker and turn onto its side to pencil in the cut line. Next, move the scribe up the rod and tilt it slightly so that the pencil is touching the egg; now draw in a second oval shape above the cut line to indicate the position of the central decorated panel on the lid. If the pencil marks don't meet up, don't worry: you can correct them freehand later. Turn the marker up the right way and pencil in two small marks front and back on the cut line to indicate the centre. Now place a small mark below the cut line in the centre, and measure an equal distance either side of the centre marks on the cut line. Join these marks up with a curving line until the V-shape looks right, then do the same with the central oval.

Mark where the hinge will go, and cut out the small post section.

Setting the hinge into an ostrich egg is a little bit more difficult than on any of the other eggs, as the outer shell is quite waxy and even the epoxy resin has a problem adhering to it. I normally score the outer shell using my small drill bit – you need to have as much 'key' as possible for the glue to stick to. Position the hinge, but don't glue just yet. While it is in position, make pencil marks in the six small holes, remove the hinge, and, using a flame drill bit, drill the holes in the shell to take the pins. Score the hinge and, using well-mixed epoxy, attach it to the shell. Before the glue sets, insert the pins, pushing them through the holes so that they are snug to the hinge. Leave to set for at least an hour before cutting the egg open.

Score the inner oval on the lid before cutting the egg open. To avoid some of the splintering that is inevitable when cutting an ostrich egg, paint a thin layer of clear nail varnish over the cutting line, and cut carefully. Once the egg has been cut open, be careful not to just let the lid sit back on the hinge, as it may snap with the weight. Trim the pins with wire cutters and bend the ends into the inside of the shell.

Cleaning the membrane from the inside is a little harder than on a goose egg. If I am lining the shell I normally just rub the inside down with glasspaper to remove any loose bits of membrane, but if you want to remove all of the membrane you can soak the whole shell in a strong, neat bleach for a few hours – don't forget about it, though, or you will just end up with a hinge and a few pins floating in the bleach! Rinse afterwards in cold water.

Fill the blowhole in the same way as you would for a goose egg, and rub down to a smooth finish when set.

Paint the base and the edge of the lid in the main colour, and the inner oval in a colour which suits your choice of transfer. For my cherub transfer I painted a sky background using acrylic paints, being careful to leave the area where the cherubs would go white, since the waterslide transfers are transparent.

Apply a generous coat of varnish to the outer edge of the lid, and while it is still wet sprinkle with the polyflakes; spray with hairspray when dry. Be careful not to get the hairspray on the paint, or it will lift; if this does happen, leave it to reset for a while.

Apply the transfer to the lid, making sure you smooth out all the air bubbles and creases before sealing with the hairdryer. Add several coats of varnish to 'sink' the transfer, rubbing down with wet-and-dry paper every few coats.

Line the inside of the egg in the same way as before; you can use satin or velvet, as you wish. Before securing the lining in place, glue in a length of chain, with epoxy resin, to stop the lid from opening too far. All lids fitted to ostrich eggs need a chain to prevent the hinge breaking.

Attach a line of the fine gold cord around the inner oval, then add a row of the crystal and pearl chain to the inside of the oval, followed by another row of the fine gold cord; a single row of the fine gold cord is added to the cut edge of the lid. For ease of opening the egg, a bow filigree is fixed to the point of the lid to act as a handle. I have used a wider contrasting braid to edge the cut line of the base, and mitred the edges.

Score the cup part of the stand with the drill bit; also score the egg where it will sit in the cup. I have a drill bit that I use only for scoring the hinges and the cups on the stands, as this saves blunting the ones I use on the eggs. With some well-mixed epoxy resin, and with small bits of tissue added for better adhesion, glue the egg to the stand. I tilted my egg forward slightly to show off the transfer on the lid.

53

PETAL CUTS

These spectacular designs open all the way around, which makes them ideal for holding a small figure or diorama. Petal-cut eggs look their best if displayed slightly open.

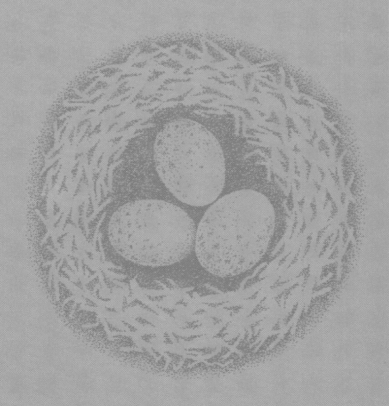

TWO-PETAL EGG

Even the most straightforward of the petal cuts makes a very imposing ornament. This design is easy to mark out, as all the cut lines are straight.

You will need the following:

- a tall goose egg
- fine-grade glasspaper
- egg marker or elastic band
- hobby drill and 3mm (⅛in) drill bit
- paints, brush and/or sponge
- two transfers
- small figure
- a filigree to serve as base for the figure
- pearl chain, or strung beads
- ultrafine polyflakes
- epoxy resin and tacky glue
- two small hinges and petroleum jelly
- two small filigrees suitable for use as hinge covers
- a selection of braids
- a low stand suitable for a goose egg.

Prepare the egg in the usual way.

Place the egg in the marker and mark in the base cut line about a quarter of the way up from the bottom, then turn the marker onto its side and divide the upper part of the egg into four sections (Fig 5.1). Two of these lines indicate the division between the petals; the others are the centre lines for the hinges and the transfers. Make a small mark on each of the petals where the transfers will sit; you must make sure that these marks are even and central.

Mark in for the hinges and cut the post area out as described on page 23; prepare and fit the hinges. When the hinges are set, cut the egg open: cut the top line first, then the lower line. Care needs to be taken when cutting the cross section; remember to score first.

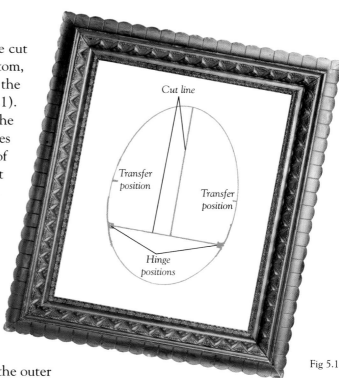

Fig 5.1

Paint the shell inside and out with base coat, and leave to dry. When the base coat is dry, give the outer shell three top coats.

Coat the insides of the petals with the water-based varnish and polyflakes, repeat if necessary, and then seal with hairspray when dry. Make a small platform, as described on page 48, for the inside of the base, and decorate to match the interior of the shell.

Fix the transfers to each petal, making sure they are both even; you will have to judge this by eye.

Decorate the outside of the shell with the braids and the pearl chain.

Glue the egg to the stand, and then glue the large filigree and the figure to the platform.

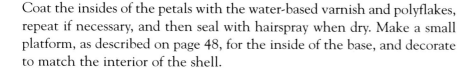

THREE-PETAL EGG

The asymmetrical petals give this design a particularly showy appearance, rather like a magnolia flower. Care is needed in the marking out, but it is not as difficult as it looks.

You will need the following:

- a tall goose egg
- fine-grade glasspaper
- egg marker or elastic band
- hobby drill and 3mm (⅛in) drill bit
- paints, brush and/or sponge
- a small figure
- three small filigrees, and another three suitable for use as hinge covers
- pearl chain
- ultrafine polyflakes
- epoxy resin and tacky glue
- three small hinges and petroleum jelly
- a selection of braids
- a low stand suitable for a goose egg.

Prepare the shell. Place the egg into the marker and mark in the base line, then turn the marker onto its side and divide the egg into 12 sections. Place a further three vertical lines above the base line, spacing them equally – in my case, about 1.5cm (⅝in) apart (Fig 5.2).

Each of the three spiral lines occupies four of the 12 sections marked on the egg. Starting from the straight base line, draw gently curving lines from corner to corner of each of the marked 'squares', meeting neatly at the top (Figs 5.3 and 5.4).

Cut line

Fig 5.2

Cut line

Hinge

Cut line

Fig 5.3

Top view

Fig 5.4

Place the hinge marks slightly off-centre as shown in Fig 5.3, and score in the filigree positions. You will have to judge the positions by eye; they need to be slightly offset to allow for the tilted shape of the petals. Cut the hinge-post sections as usual, and attach the hinges. Once set, carefully cut the egg open, remembering that you are less likely to break the egg if you score all of the lines prior to cutting.

Soak the shell to remove the membrane, fill the blowhole and rub down to a flush finish.

Make a small platform for the inside of the base, as before.

Paint the inside of the shell with your chosen colour and then, when dry, coat with the varnish and polyflakes; when completely dry, seal with hairspray.

Paint the outer shell, and then glue the filigrees into position using the score marks as a guide.

Decorate the edges of the petals with the gold cord and pearl chain, attach the egg to the stand and add the figure to the inside. This egg is best displayed with the petals slightly open.

FOUR-PETAL
FLOWER BASKET

This unusually ornate design features two eggs, one inside the other, with elaborately shaped cut-outs in each. It is not especially difficult to make, but requires patience and a steady hand.

You will need the following:

- a tall goose egg
- a small duck egg
- fine-grade glasspaper
- egg marker or elastic band
- hobby drill with 3mm (⅛in) drill bit and flame drill bit
- paints, brush and/or sponge
- filigree to use as a base for the duck egg
- a selection of small silk flowers
- four small waterslide transfers
- ultrafine polyflakes
- epoxy resin and tacky glue
- a decorator's filler such as Polyfilla
- four small hinges and petroleum jelly
- four small filigrees suitable for hinge covers
- a selection of braids
- a low stand suitable for a goose egg.

Prepare both of the eggs in the usual way.

GOOSE EGG

Place the egg into the marker and draw in the base line, then turn the marker onto its side and then divide the egg into quarters. Turn the marker upright and draw in a further two lines above the base line, depending on the size of the transfers (Fig 5.5). Remove the egg from the marker and draw in a border around each of the petals, about 5mm (about ¼in) inside the cut lines – for accuracy, you will need to use a tape measure and measure all of the way around each of the petals on either side of the cut lines.

Using the two horizontal lines above the base line as a guide, draw around the trimmed waterslide transfers, keeping them in the same place on each petal.

Mark and cut for the hinges, glue the hinges into position and leave to set.

Using the flame drill bit, cut around the transfer marks. Change drill bits and score the rest of the cut lines in the usual way. Cut out the inner sections first and then, very carefully, cut the petals open.

To clean the membrane from this type of egg I always soak it in a solution of bleach, but don't leave the egg in the bleach for too long or you will end up with nothing but hinges!

Fill the blowhole and, when set, rub down to a flush finish.

This type of egg almost always needs to be reinforced. Mix a small amount of epoxy resin and add some polyflakes to the mixture. Working quickly, coat the insides of the petals one at a time; discard the mixture if it starts to set, or you will end up with jagged bits of glue sticking out from the shell. Make a small platform for the base of the egg and glue into position. Treat the inside of the base in the same way as the petals, then leave to set.

Paint the outer shell with two coats of the base colour and, when dry, paint with the top coat. Add the transfers to each of the petals.

Paint the borders of the petals with the water-based varnish and, while still wet, sprinkle with the polyflakes; avoid painting over the transfers.

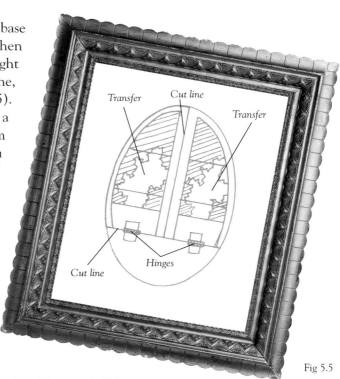

Fig 5.5

Treat the base of the egg in the same way. Repeat if necessary and seal with hairspray.

Glue the egg to the stand, and add fine gold cord to all of the cut edges, and hinge covers to each of the hinges.

DUCK EGG

Place the egg into the marker and divide into 12 sections. Turn the marker upright and draw a line around the lower part of the egg and another slightly above the first; you will need a further line above the first two, and another passing over the top of the egg (Fig 5.6). Remove the egg from the marker and, using a tape measure, measure 4mm (³⁄₁₆in) either side of one of the vertical lines going all of the way around the egg, and join these marks up to give the outline of the basket handle. Mark in the scallops round the base and the scalloped shape of the handle, then cut out the shaded areas. Carefully score and then cut the scrap pieces of egg away.

You should not need to remove the membrane from the inside of the shell unless it is extremely dirty. Fill the blowhole and, when set, rub down to a flush finish.

Reinforce the inside of the shell in the same way as you did the goose egg, and leave to set.

Fig 5.6

Paint the outer shell and then coat with the water-based varnish and polyflakes. Trim the cut edges with the fine gold cord and add the filigree to the bottom of the egg to act as a base.

Arrange the small flowers into a miniature bouquet, fill the bottom of the duck egg with filler, push the bouquet into this and leave to set.

Finally, glue the flower basket to the inside of the goose egg.

CHAPTER 6

Eggs with doors

I must admit I do enjoy doing this type of egg. Eggs with shaped openings, with or without the doors, also make lovely tree decorations at Christmas if you add an up-eye to the top and some ribbon or chain for hanging.

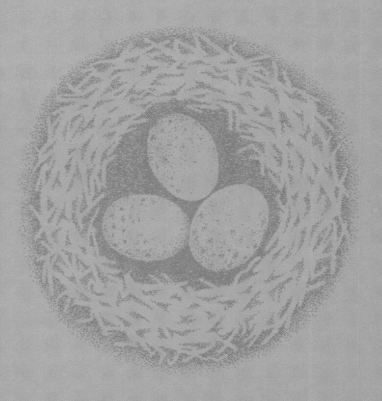

SINGLE-DOOR EGG

The door in this delicate design is decorated with a cut-out using the same technique as the previous project.

You will need the following:

- a fat goose egg
- fine-grade glasspaper
- egg marker or elastic band
- hobby drill with 3mm (⅛in) drill bit and flame bit
- paints, brush and/or sponge
- ultrafine polyflakes, golden tint
- epoxy resin and tacky glue
- small hinge and petroleum jelly
- filigree suitable for a hinge cover
- small waterslide transfer or Mamelock scrap (used in découpage)
- water-based varnish
- a selection of braids and beads
- small figure or ornament to go inside the egg
- components to make a handle (optional)
- a stand suitable for a goose egg
- material to line the inside of the egg (optional).

Prepare the egg in the usual way. Find the centre of its height, and make a small pencil mark. Place the egg in the marker and pencil in the centre line, then turn the marker on its side, move the pencil up the scribe and tilt it to touch the egg; this allows you to draw in the oval for the door. Draw another oval inside the first; this will be the border.

Remove the egg from the marker and, using the centre line as a guide, mark for the hinge and also where you want the handle (if you are adding one) to sit. Cut the post area out as usual and attach the hinge.

Place the trimmed transfer (do not remove the backing at this stage) or trimmed scrap onto the door of the egg, making sure that it overlaps the border in at least three places, and draw around it.

Using the flame drill bit, cut around the pencil marks where the scrap will sit, then change bits and cut out the excess egg within the border (Fig 6.1). Next, carefully cut the door open.

To clean the membrane from the inside of the shell, you might find it easier to soak the egg in lukewarm water for about 10 minutes to loosen it. The only problem with soaking the shell is that you have to wait several hours for it to dry out before you can paint it, but the membrane normally comes away in one piece when you do it this way.

Handle position (optional)

Fig 6.1

Fill the blowhole, and rub down flush with the egg when set.

Paint the shell inside and out with the base paint, and leave to dry thoroughly before painting with the top coat. Make a small platform (see page 48) to fit the bottom of the shell and glue into position.

Paint the inside of the shell and reinforce the inside of the door with the water-based varnish and whilst still wet sprinkle with the polyflakes; when dry, repeat this process, sealing the final coat with hairspray.

Paint the back of the scrap with the water-based varnish, attach it to the door and leave to dry; or, if you are using a waterslide transfer, attach it in the usual way. Once the scrap is dry, carefully paint in the border with the water-based varnish and sprinkle with the polyflakes; repeat when set, then use hairspray to seal.

Decorate the outer shell with braids and beads, glue the small figure to the inside of the shell, attach the hinge covers, and the handle if required. Glue the egg to the stand.

THREE-DOOR EGG

The distinctive feature of this design is the Paisley-shaped doors which do not fill more than half the opening, so the interior is still visible even when the doors are closed.

You will need the following:

- a goose egg
- fine-grade glasspaper
- egg marker or elastic band
- hobby drill and 3mm (⅛in) drill bit
- paints, brush and/or sponge
- ultrafine polyflakes
- epoxy resin and tacky glue
- three small hinges and petroleum jelly
- filigrees suitable for use as hinge covers
- water-based varnish
- fine gold cord
- pearl and crystal chain
- a small figure or ornament to go inside the egg
- material for handles: up-eyes, chain, drop beads, six jump rings, pins
- a stand suitable for an upright goose egg.

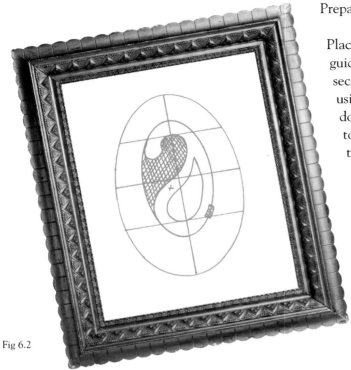

Fig 6.2

Prepare the egg in the usual way.

Place the egg in the marker and pencil in the guidelines shown in Fig 6.2. Divide the egg into three sections using the marker or a tape measure, and, using the drawn lines as a guide, mark out the three doors. Mark for the hinges; I have placed them towards the bottom of the doors, but you could put them in the centre if you wished.

Cut the hinge-post sections from the shell, and score in the rest of the cut lines, and where the handles will sit. Use the finishing paper to remove any unnecessary pencil marks. Glue the hinges in place and, when set, cut the doors open, cutting away the shaded area first.

Clean the membrane from the inside of the egg and fill the blowhole; when dry, rub down to a flush finish.

Now paint the outer shell; I used matt acrylic followed by Duncan's pearl sheen.

Paint in the borders of the doors with the water-based varnish and, while this is still wet, sprinkle with polyflakes; repeat as many times as necessary to achieve the desired finish.

Make a small platform for the inside of the egg and glue it into position, paint the inside with the water based varnish and whilst still wet sprinkle with the polyflakes, seal with hairspray when it is dry. To strengthen the doors I coated them with epoxy resin, followed by polyflakes.

Trim the outer shell with the fine gold cord, and decorate with the pearl and crystal chain and gold cord. Use well-mixed epoxy resin to glue the egg to the stand.

Glue the figure to the inside of the shell. Attach the handles and the hinge covers, making sure that they are all even.

EMU EGG WITH THREE HEXAGONAL DOORS

This kind of design has many possibilities: it is large enough to hold multiple figures or quite a complex scene.

You will need the following:

- an emu or rhea egg
- fine-grade glasspaper
- egg marker or elastic band
- hobby drill and 3mm (⅛in) drill bit
- paints, Diamond Shimmer, brush and/or sponge
- epoxy resin and tacky glue
- three small hinges and petroleum jelly
- filigrees suitable for use as hinge covers
- fine gold cord
- picot-edged braid
- pearl chain
- components to make up three handles: up-eyes, chain, drop beads, six jump rings, pins
- three small angels to go inside the egg
- a stand suitable for an upright emu or rhea egg.

When preparing these larger eggs, do not rub the shell too much, as you do not want to lose the natural markings; rub it just enough to give a key for the paint.

Place the egg into the marker and divide into 12 sections; mark in the doors, hinge marks and handle positions (Fig 6.3).

Cut for the hinge posts and score all of the other marks; attach the hinges and, when set, cut open the doors.

As I have said earlier, the easiest way to remove the membrane from the inside of the larger shells is to soak them in a solution of bleach and water – but do remember that if you leave it in the solution for too long the shell will dissolve.

Paint the shell inside and out, make a platform for the inside and paint to match the interior of the shell. When the inside is dry, coat several times with diamond shimmer or, if you prefer, coat with varnish and polyflakes.

Apply the fine gold cord to the outside and inside of the doors, and then add picot-edged braid. Use gold cord and pearl chain to decorate around the doors, add the handles to each of the doors, and leave to set.

I applied several coats of Diamond Shimmer to the wings of the angels before installing them in the shell.

Glue the egg to the stand.

Fig 6.3

CHAPTER

ENLARGING THE SHELL

This treatment is ideal if you have an awkwardly shaped figure or ornament that won't fit into a normal egg. It does take a little practice to get the placement of the filigrees just right, but persevere, as these eggs are gorgeous.

SINGLE HEART ENLARGEMENT

The heart shape projecting from the back of this egg reflects the theme of the happy couple shown inside.

You will need the following:

- a tall goose egg
- fine-grade glasspaper
- egg marker or elastic band
- hobby drill with 3mm (⅛in) drill bit and flame bit
- paints, brush and/or sponge
- two waterslide transfers
- peel-off rose transfer
- four small S-shaped filigrees
- figures to go inside the egg
- epoxy resin and tacky glue
- a selection of braids
- a stand suitable for a goose egg.

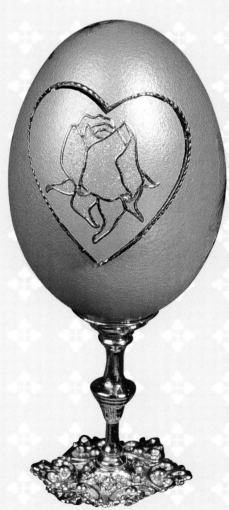

Prepare the egg shell and place into the marker; mark in an oval on the front of the egg and a heart on the back (Fig 7.1).

Trim the waterslide transfers and, using the drawn oval as a guide, place them on the shell. Draw around the trimmed edge where the transfers overlap the inside of the oval (Fig 7.2). Cut out the heart shape from the back of the shell, and the inner part of the oval; use the flame bit to follow the drawn lines around the waterslide transfers.

Back

Fig 7.1

Front

Fig 7.2

Clean the inside of the shell and, when it is dry, fill the blowhole; leave to set and then rub down to a flush finish.

Paint the egg and the heart cut-out, both inside and out. Leave to dry, then attach the waterslide transfers to the front opening. Trim the peel-off transfer and attach to the heart-shaped piece.

Glue the small S-shaped filigrees into position on the heart-shaped opening at the back of the shell; when set, glue the heart-shaped piece to the filigrees, as shown in the side-view photograph.

Make a small platform to fit inside the bottom of the shell for the figures to stand on, and paint to match the interior of the shell. Fix into position and, when dry, attach the figures. Finally, glue the egg to the stand.

TRIPLE OVAL
ENLARGEMENT

T he side openings in this egg match the shape of the front opening, so the finished piece looks attractive and harmonious from all angles.

You will need the following:

- a tall, fat goose egg
- fine-grade glasspaper
- egg marker or elastic band
- hobby drill and 3mm (⅛in) drill bit
- paints, brush and/or sponge
- ultrafine polyflakes
- two ballerina filigrees
- 16 small S-shaped filigrees
- small ballerina figure to go inside
- epoxy resin and tacky glue
- fine gold cord
- picot-edged cord
- a stand suitable for a goose egg.

Score edge of painted border

Cut lines

Filigree

Fig 7.3

Prepare the egg in the usual way. Place into the marker and pencil in the guidelines. Then mark in three ovals using the method described on page 69; these will need to be quite large. Next, mark in smaller ovals inside two of the larger ones, making sure that the ballerina filigrees will sit on the outer edges of the smaller ovals when cut out (as the transfers do on the Four-Petal Flower Basket and the Single-Door Egg). Mark out the scalloped border between the two outer ovals (Fig 7.3).

Carefully cut the egg. First lightly score the scalloped border outline, then cut out the small ovals and finally the three larger ones. Don't throw away the cut-outs, as you never know when you may find a use for them.

Clean the inside of the egg and the cut-outs you will be using, fill the blowhole and, when set, rub down to a flush finish.

Paint the outside of the shell, but not the border; also paint the oval cut-outs in the main colour. When the outer shell is dry, paint the inner borders, the inside of the egg and the insides of the oval cut-outs in a contrasting colour. I have used black as my main colour and gold for the contrast, as this will show off the golden-tint polyflakes to their best.

Make a small platform to go into the bottom of the egg for the figure to stand on, and glue this into position; when set, paint to match the inside of the egg.

Coat the inside of the egg and the insides of the oval cut-outs with several coats of water-based varnish and polyflakes; when thoroughly dry, coat the inner borders in the same way.

Apply the picot-edged braid to all the oval edges, including the inner ovals on the side extensions. Use the fine gold cord to outline the outer border, and the rest of the cut edges on the oval cut-outs.

Glue the egg to the stand and, when set, glue the figure to the inside of the egg. Attach the S-shaped filigrees to the main body of the egg; when set, attach the oval cut-outs, completing one side at a time. Once the cut-outs are set into position you can add the ballerina filigrees.

ENLARGED EGG WITH REVERSED HEARTS

This egg is enlarged in two stages, with the outer pieces reversed to show their concave side: an elaborate design suitable for a special occasion.

You will need the following:

- a tall, fat goose egg
- fine-grade glasspaper
- egg marker or elastic band
- hobby drill and 3mm (⅛in) drill bit
- paints, brush and/or sponge
- ultrafine polyflakes
- eight small S-shaped filigrees
- two small rose filigrees
- a figure to go inside the egg
- epoxy resin and tacky glue
- picot-edged braid
- a stand suitable for a goose egg.

Prepare the egg in the usual way. Place into the egg marker and mark in three large ovals, then smaller ovals inside two of the larger ones, and finally hearts inside the two smaller ovals.

Cut out the hearts first, then the ovals. Clean the membrane from the shell and fill the blowhole, rubbing down to a flush finish when dry.

Make a small cardboard platform for the inside of the egg and glue this into position.

Paint the egg, the oval cut-outs, the hearts and the inside of the egg in the main colour. Paint the insides of the hearts (that is, the concave side, which will be outside when finished) in a contrasting colour. When the inside is dry, apply several coats of water-based varnish and polyflakes.

Glue the picot-edged braid to all of the cut edges on the egg and the four cut-outs.

Attach the S-shaped filigrees to the ovals and, when set, glue the oval cut-outs into position.

Glue the hearts to the ovals, reversing them as shown, then add the small rose filigrees.

Glue the egg to the stand and then glue the figures to the inside.

CHAPTER 8

LATTICEWORK

There are several different ways to achieve a lattice effect on the shell. The first method described is by far the easiest that I have found, even if it does take ages to cut out the strips of paper; the easiest way to do this is with a paper cutter and cutting mat, if you have these. The floral latticework is very labour-intensive but the finished result is well worth the effort.

BASIC
LATTICE-CUT EGG

T he lattice here forms a patterned background to the figure. Accuracy
is essential in the marking of this egg, and for best results I would
suggest using an egg marker.

You will need the following:

- a tall, fat goose egg
- fine-grade glasspaper,
- egg marker
- hobby drill with flame bit and
  3mm (⅛in) drill bit
- paints, brush and/or sponge
- four waterslide transfers
- a figure to go inside the egg
- ultrafine polyflakes
- epoxy resin and tacky glue
- strips of paper 5mm (³⁄₁₆in) wide
- a stand suitable for a goose egg.

Prepare the egg in the usual way, place into the marker and mark in an oval. Mark in the centre girth line, then a line 1cm (⅜in) above and another the same distance below the centre line. Mark in vertical lines all of the way around the egg.

Cut the excess paper from the waterslide transfers, position them on the egg around the oval and draw around them; this will mark the limit of the lattice-cut area.

Divide the middle section of the egg into squares, using a tape measure and the egg marker, and mark all the diagonals (Fig 8.1). Then use the water-based varnish to glue the strips of paper over the graphed lines.

Cut out the lattice section with the 3mm (⅛in) drill bit and then cut out the main opening with the flame bit.

Clean the inside of the egg and remove the strips of paper; after soaking the egg in warm water for about 10 minutes, the paper can be gently rubbed away. Fill the blowhole and, when dry, rub down to a flush finish.

Make a small platform for the inside of the egg and glue into position.

Paint the inside and outside of the egg. When dry, give the inside of the shell several coats of water-based varnish and polyflakes.

Attach the waterslide transfers around the front opening of the egg.

Apply the gold cord to the latticework to give the impression of interwoven fencing (Fig 8.2), then add picot-edged braid to the top and bottom borders of the latticework.

Glue the figure to the inside of the egg and then glue the egg to the stand.

Back view

Fig 8.1

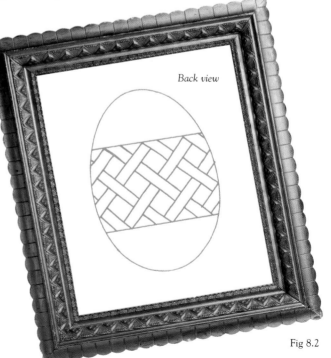

Back view

Fig 8.2

TRIPLE HEART AND FLORAL LATTICEWORK

This complex design combines floral latticework with a variant of the shell-enlargement technique introduced in the previous chapter.

You will need the following:

- a tall, fat goose egg
- fine-grade glasspaper
- egg marker
- hobby drill, flame bit and 3mm (⅛in) drill bit
- paints, brush and/or sponge
- a figure to go inside the egg
- two small rose filigrees
- ultrafine polyflakes
- epoxy resin and tacky glue
- fine gold cord
- fine pearl chain
- a stand suitable for a goose egg.

Prepare the egg in the usual way, place into the egg marker and graph the shell with vertical centre lines. Remove from the marker and draw in three hearts, evenly spaced around the egg. Next draw in three further hearts, 5mm (³⁄₁₆in) smaller, inside the first three (Fig 8.3).

Divide the shell into squares, using the egg marker, and draw in the diagonals all over the shell (except from inside the hearts). When the whole of the egg has been marked up in this way, draw small circles over the diamond shapes as shown in Fig 8.4; the shaded areas will be cut out.

Fig 8.3

Fig 8.4

Score around the inner hearts with the 3mm (⅛in) drill bit, then with the flame bit cut out the floral latticework: insert the point of the flame drill into the egg and guide it around the shaded area so you are left with little flower shapes. When all of the latticework is cut, you can then cut out the inner hearts.

It is not advisable to try and clean the inside of the shell; instead, gently rub away the loose bits of membrane with small pieces of sandpaper, fill the blowhole and, when dry, rub down to a smooth finish.

Make a small platform for the inside of the egg and glue into position, then paint the egg inside and out, and paint the hearts.

Coat the inside of the egg and the hearts with several coats of water-based varnish and polyflakes.

Apply two rows of the fine gold cord around the front heart, then add a row of the fine pearl chain, followed by a further two rows of the fine gold cord. The other two hearts are lined with six rows of the fine gold cord.

Glue the figure to the inside of the egg.

The heart cut-outs are outlined with the fine gold cord and a row of the fine pearl chain, and their insides are lined with a single row of the fine gold cord. A small rose filigree is glued to the outside of each of the hearts, which are then glued to the shell slightly below the cut line.

Finally, glue the egg to the stand and, if you wish, add a base as described on page 24.

FLORAL
LATTICE PANEL

An unusually elaborate front opening is the distinguishing feature of
this dainty design.

You will need the following:

- a tall, fat goose egg
- fine-grade glasspaper
- egg marker or elastic band
- hobby drill, flame bit and 3mm (⅛in) drill bit
- paints, brush and/or sponge
- a figure to go inside the egg
- four scroll filigrees
- ultrafine polyflakes
- epoxy resin and tacky glue
- fine gold cord
- pearl and crystal chain
- a stand suitable for a goose egg.

Prepare the egg in the usual way, place into the marker and divide the shell into squares as before. The outlines of the cut-out section and the latticework at the back are very similar to the borders on the Triple Oval Enlargement egg in Chapter 7. Bend the scroll filigrees so that they will fit snugly to the shell and then draw around them; the shaded areas in Fig 8.5 will be cut away.

In the back panel, mark in for the floral latticework (Fig 8.6) and cut this section first, remembering to score the outline beforehand.

Fig 8.5

Fig 8.6

Cut out the shaded areas on the front, then cut out the main opening. Carefully remove any loose bits of membrane from the inside of the shell with small pieces of sandpaper, fill the blowhole and, when dry, rub down to a smooth finish.

Paint the shell inside and out. Make a small platform to fit inside, and glue into position. Coat the inside with water-based varnish and polyflakes.

Glue the filigrees into position and, when set, add the gold cord and crystal chain to the inner section of shell, and gold cord to the outer cut sections. Apply a row of gold cord, followed by a row of the pearl and crystal chain, to the floral lattice section at the back of the egg, and finish off with a final row of the gold cord.

Glue the egg to the stand and then glue the figure inside.

CLOCKS

These eggs are always popular, and with a little practice quite quick to make. The first two are very similar in the materials used, but adding several coats of polyflakes to the outer shell makes the finished results quite different.

GOOSE-EGG CLOCK

T he dark colour and restrained decoration give this clock a rather classical, almost Regency flavour.

You will need the following:

- a tall, fat goose egg
- fine-grade glasspaper
- egg marker or elastic band
- hobby drill and 3mm (⅛in) drill bit
- paints, brush and/or sponge
- small quartz clock movement with removable cup
- two scroll filigrees, one left-hand, one right-hand
- long leaf filigree
- two small bow filigrees
- crystal and pearl chain
- fine gold cord
- high-gloss spirit-based varnish
- epoxy resin and tacky glue
- a stand suitable for a goose egg.

Prepare the egg in the usual way.

Measure the back of the clock cup and make a template from thick card (Fig 9.1). Use this to mark on the egg where the cut-out for the clock will be; you want it slightly above the centre of the egg.

Cut out the small circle. Now, chances are that the opening will seem too small for the cup to sit in, so keep trimming around the opening and trying the cup until it fits inside the opening. Take your time, and be careful you don't trim away too much shell, or the cup will just fall inside the egg. The lip of the cup should sit snugly against the egg at the top and bottom of the opening.

Clean the inside of the egg and fill the blowhole; when, dry rub down to a smooth finish, and paint the egg.

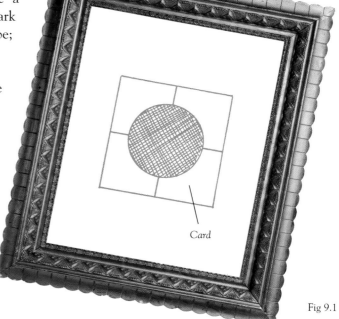

Card

Fig 9.1

Allow plenty of drying time before giving the egg several coats of gloss varnish; ideally you should leave at least six hours between coats of varnish and rub down every three coats with wet-and-dry paper before giving a final coat of varnish.

Glue the egg to the stand and leave to set.

Using well-mixed epoxy, glue the cup into the opening, making sure that it is sitting in straight, that the little section for the winder is to the right, and the clock will sit straight in the cup.

Insert the clock into the cup, and add a row of the crystal and pearl chain around the clock using tacky glue, making sure that it is even all the way round. Add a row of the fine gold cord and then repeat with the pearl and crystal chain, and finally two rows of the gold cord.

Bend the scroll filigrees so they will sit against the shell, and then glue into position with well-mixed epoxy, keeping them even on both sides of the shell. Glue one of the bows to the top of the shell, in between the two scrolls.

Bend the long leaf filigree so it will fit the curve of the shell below the clock, and glue it into position, making sure that it is straight; then glue the other small bow filigree to the centre of the leaf filigree.

GLITTERING GOOSE-EGG CLOCK

This more ornate version of the same design features a wide base to add stability.

You will need the following:

- a tall, fat goose egg
- fine-grade glasspaper
- egg marker or elastic band
- hobby drill and 3mm (⅛in) drill bit
- paints, brush and/or sponge
- small quartz clock movement with removable cup
- two long filigrees
- pearl chain
- crystal floral chain
- ultrafine polyflakes
- fine gold cord
- base
- epoxy resin and tacky glue
- a stand suitable for a goose egg.

Prepare the egg in the usual way.

Mark and cut the hole for the clock cup exactly as before.

Clean the inside of the egg and fill the blowhole; when dry, rub down to a smooth finish.

Give the egg and base two or three coats of acrylic paint to cover any blemishes, and leave to dry; then coat the whole shell several times with water-based varnish and ultrafine polyflakes, finishing with hairspray to seal the final coat.

Paint the contrasting band around the base, and then coat the inner and outer sections with the water-based varnish and the ultrafine polyflakes. Apply a row of fine gold cord to the edges of the band, and then glue a row of the crystal floral chain to the centre of the band.

Glue the egg to the stand and leave to set.

Using well-mixed epoxy, glue the cup into the opening, making sure that it is sitting in straight, that the little section for the winder is to the right, and that the clock will sit straight in the cup.

Place the clock into the cup and add rows of pearl chain, gold cord, crystal floral chain, gold cord, pearl chain and finally another row of the gold cord around the clock face.

Bend the filigrees so that they will sit neatly on the shell, then paint them to match the colours used on the base. When dry, glue the filigrees to the shell above and below the clock. If you want to paint the filigrees, always bend them first; the paint will crack if you try to bend them afterwards.

Finally, glue the stand to the base.

OSTRICH-EGG CLOCK WITH REAR DOORS

This large, imposing clock would be ideal for the mantelpiece of even the most formal of rooms. Distinctively shaped doors at the back provide access to the clock mechanism.

You will need the following:

- An ostrich egg
- fine-grade glasspaper
- egg marker or elastic band
- hobby drill, flame bit and drill bits suitable for cutting an ostrich egg
- paints, brush and/or sponge
- two large hinges with holes and six pins
- filigrees suitable for use as hinge covers
- quartz clock movement
- crystal floral chain
- fine gold cord
- picot-edged braid
- three large waterslide transfers
- epoxy resin and tacky glue
- satin to line the egg
- a stand suitable for an ostrich egg.

Rub down the egg just enough to give a key for the paint.

Make a template for the clock and mark the opening as before; it is best to have the clock face fairly central on an ostrich egg. Mark a larger circle in the back, just big enough to get your hand in, and mark in a 'Yin and Yang' shape for the two doors (Fig 9.2). Pencil in the hinge marks and cut out the post area, score the shell where the hinges will sit and mark for the pins. With the flame drill bit, drill the holes for the pins; then glue the hinges into position and push the pins through the holes.

Cut out the opening for the clock face, trimming until the clock sits neatly inside the opening. Cut open the doors in the back, then trim the pins and bend them flat against the shell.

Rub away the loose bits of membrane with sandpaper, fill the blowhole and, when dry, rub down to a flush finish.

Fig 9.2

Paint the egg, and also paint about 1cm (⅜in) inside the cut edges of the shell, including on the doors.

Glue the egg to the stand, and leave to set.

To line the inside of this egg you will need to make a large tube of material; the larger the tube, the more gathered the lining will be. First of all, measure from the clock opening to the doors on the inside of the shell and add 6cm (about 2½in); this is the width of the piece of material you will cut. The length determines the size of the tube, so the longer your piece of material, the bigger the tube – I cut mine 90cm (3ft) long!

The lining is made up in almost the same way as for the Casket-Cut Egg in Chapter 3. On one of the short ends glue in a hem, and then secure this to the opposite short end with more glue to make a tube. Using a close running stitch, stitch along both ends of the tube so that they can be gathered. Next gather one end so it will fit inside the clock opening; place a line of glue close to the cut edge of the opening and secure the lining into position. Gather the other end to fit inside the opening for the doors, and again glue into the egg close to the edge. Apply a row of braid to each of the openings to hide the gathered edges.

To line the doors you will need to cut a large circle of material and then cut it to match the 'Yin and Yang' shape of the doors. Gather to fit each of the doors, and glue into position, adding braid to the outer edges; remember not to take the braid too close to the edge of the door, or the doors won't close properly.

With some well-mixed epoxy, glue the clock into position, making sure it is straight. Apply a row of the floral crystal chain around the clock face, then add a row of the fine gold cord, followed by a row of the picot-edged braid. Add the waterslide transfers, and seal them with several coats of water-based varnish.

Decorate the outsides of the doors with the fine gold cord and picot-edged braid. I made the handles out of pieces of costume jewellery from a charity shop.

HINGE RINGS

The addition of a hinge ring to the egg can have a stunning effect. There are many different ways to fit a hinge ring, but the method described in this chapter is the easiest that I have found. It is important that the egg fits the hinge ring, as you will not be able to force the shell into the ring; always measure the circumference (girth) of the egg with a tape measure and then choose a suitable ring to fit.

A BASIC
HINGE-RING EGG

The brightly lacquered hinge ring provides a contrasting accent to this tastefully understated design.

You will need the following items:

- A goose egg, approx. 18cm (7in) in circumference
- 5.7cm (2¼in) hinge ring
- egg marker or elastic band
- hobby drill and 3mm (⅛in) drill bit, or craft knife
- paint and brush or sponge
- water-based varnish
- epoxy resin and tacky glue
- small waterslide transfers
- fine gold cord
- braid with scalloped edges
- ultrafine polyflakes, 'aurora'
- material to line the inside of the shell
- a low stand suitable for a goose egg.

First, you need to establish the exact point on the surface of the egg where its circumference matches that of the hinge ring. To do this, place a thin line of tacky glue around the inner edge of the hinge ring and glue the fine gold cord into position. Mark with a dark pen where one end meets the other, then remove the cord from the hinge ring and cut at the mark. Tape the two ends together, making sure that the ends do not overlap. This loop of cord is your guide to measure the egg where the cut line will be; place it carefully to one side.

Prepare the eggshell in the usual way, then take your 'guide' that you made earlier and place it around the shell, making sure it is straight all the way round. Make a small pencil mark at this position, remove the guide, and then, using either the marker or an elastic band, mark in the cut line.

Cut the egg open, clean the membrane from the inside and, when dry, fill the blowhole; when the filler has set, rub down to a flush finish.

Paint the top and bottom of the shell, and when it is dry, line the inside using the circular method of lining (see page 11). Attach a row of the scallop-edged braid to the sewn edge.

With some well-mixed epoxy resin, first glue one half of the egg to the hinge ring; when that has set, mix some more epoxy and glue the other half into position.

Paint the base with a coat of water-based varnish and then sprinkle with the polyflakes; repeat until you are happy with the coverage. Seal the final coat with hairspray, being careful not to spray the top of the egg.

Glue the egg to the stand and leave to set.

Add the waterslide transfers to the lid; I have used six small violet transfers. I found it easier to position them evenly by looking down from the top of the egg.

Attach a row of the scallop-edged braid to the top and bottom of the shell where it meets the hinge ring.

ANNIVERSARY EGG

This is an egg that I made for my parents' ruby wedding anniversary. The letters and numbers are cut out and backed with a contrasting fabric. By changing the colour and the number in the central cameo the design could be adapted to suit any anniversary.

You will need the following:

- An ostrich egg, approx. 38cm (15in) in circumference
- hinge ring to fit; in my case, 12cm (4¾in) diameter
- egg marker
- hobby drill, with bits suitable for cutting an ostrich egg
- paint and brush or sponge
- epoxy resin and tacky glue
- fine gold cord
- ultrafine polyflakes
- pearl chain
- rat-tail braid
- fine gold cord
- material to line the inside of the egg; I used a heavy satin organza to back the cut-outs
- a stand suitable for an ostrich egg.

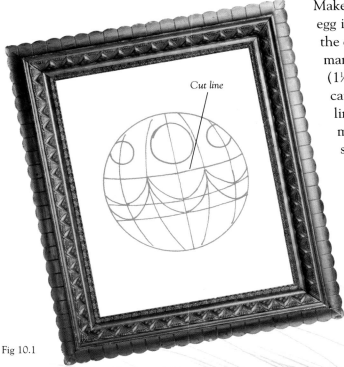

Cut line

Fig 10.1

Make a guide for the hinge ring, as before. Prepare the egg in the usual way. Using the guide, measure where the cut line will be, place the egg into the marker and mark in the cut line. Mark another line about 4cm (1½in) above the cut line, for the centres of the cameo circles, and a further two lines below the cut line to indicate the depth of the swags. Turn the marker onto its side and mark out the egg into 12 sections, then remove the egg from the marker.

Using these graph lines as a guide, mark in the three cameo circles (a larger one in the centre and smaller ones either side), then the six swags or scallops around the bottom half of the shell (Fig 10.1). Draw in the initials in the smaller cameos and the number in the central one. You might find it easier to work out the letters and numbers on paper first: they need to be designed so that there are no enclosed spaces which would fall out when the shapes are cut.

Lightly score in all of the cameos and the scallops, and carefully cut out the initials and the numbers; then cut the egg open.

Clean away the excess membrane with glasspaper, fill the blowhole and, when dry, rub down to a flush finish.

Paint the outer shell all over. When the paint is dry, coat the cameos and the scallops with water-based varnish and polyflakes.

Using the fine gold cord, outline the initials and the numbers in the cameos.

Back the cameos with a layer of organza and then a layer of your chosen lining material. Cut out pieces of material to fit just around the cut-out sections of the shell, brush tacky glue onto the inside and press the material into position.

Line the inside of both the top and bottom halves of the shell, finishing off with a row of braid to cover the sewn edge of the lining.

Glue the egg to the hinge ring.

Using the rat-tail braid and the pearl chain, outline the cameos, the scallops, and around the edge of the hinge ring.

Glue the egg to the stand.

HINGE-RING CLOCK

This imposing clock has no opening lid; instead, the hinge ring is used to hinge the clock face to the shell.

You will need the following:

- An ostrich egg
- 6.7cm (2⅝in) hinge ring
- 63mm (2½in) clock
- egg marker
- hobby drill, with bits suitable for cutting an ostrich egg
- paint and brush or sponge
- epoxy resin and tacky glue
- three large waterslide transfers
- fine gold cord
- gold strung beads
- gold looped braid
- pearl and crystal chain
- fine gold cord
- material to line the inside of the egg
- a stand suitable for an ostrich egg.

Draw around the inner edge of the hinge ring onto a piece of card and cut out the inner section; this will be the template for the hinge-ring hole, which is cut in the same way as for the goose-egg clocks (see Fig 9.1).

Prepare the egg in the usual way. Place into the marker and mark in the centre line, then turn the marker onto its side and mark in a single vertical line. Remove the egg from the marker and, using your template, mark in for the hinge ring, lining up the lines on the template with those on the egg.

Cut out the circle from the egg and trim to fit the hinge ring; you can either have the hinge to the top of the cut-out or to the left, but it must be central.

Clean the excess membrane from the inside of the shell and fill the blowhole; when it is dry, rub down to a flush finish.

Paint the outside of the shell and, when the paint is dry, line the inside using the circular method of lining, attaching a row of cord to the sewn edge.

With some well-mixed epoxy resin, glue the hinge ring to the inside of the circle so that one of the two rings sits inside the shell.

Using tacky glue, fix a row of the gold strung beads around the outer edge of the hinge ring, followed by a row of gold cord, pearl and crystal chain, and finally a row of the looped gold cord.

Trim the excess from the waterslide transfers and attach them to the outer shell, positioning them in a balanced way around the hinge ring; make sure you remove all of the air bubbles and creases before sealing with a hairdryer.

Glue the egg to the stand.

Mix some epoxy resin and, with the egg in an upright position and the hinge ring at eye level, glue the clock face into the hinge ring, making sure that 12 is at the top. When the clock face is set, glue a row of the pearl and crystal chain around the clock where it sits in the hinge ring.

EGGS WITH A DIFFERENCE

The eggs in this chapter make a nice change from the trinket boxes that are usually made. The baby carriage and the crib make ideal christening gifts, and the bells lend themselves nicely to Christmas decorations, especially if a festive musical movement is fitted.

TEAPOT

This novelty item makes an intriguing conversation piece. It is quite possible to make a whole tea set in this style, and you may even be able to think of other commonplace objects which lend themselves to this treatment.

You will need the following:

- a tall, fat goose egg
- fine-grade glasspaper
- egg marker or elastic band
- hobby drill and 3mm (⅛in) bit
- paints, brush and/or sponge
- two waterslide transfers
- spout and handle
- small hinge
- filigrees for the top of the lid
- fine gold cord
- epoxy resin and tacky glue
- large filigree to use as the base of the teapot.

Prepare the egg in the usual way. Place the egg into the marker and mark in a line about ⅔ of the way up for the lid, and a further line about ⅓ from the bottom, which is the guideline for the bottom of the spout and the handle. Next, turn the marker onto its side and mark in a line front and back. Remove the egg from the marker, mark for the hinge, and on the same side mark for the handle. Pencil in a small mark on the opposite side for the spout (Fig 11.1). Cut out the post area for the hinge and score in the small guide marks for the spout and handle. Glue the hinge into position and, when set, cut the egg open.

Clean the inside of the egg and fill the blowhole; when dry, rub down to a flush finish.

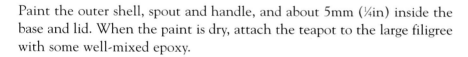

Fig 11.1

With some well-mixed epoxy, attach the spout and handle to the egg. Do these one at a time, and as the glue sets nudge the spout or handle as necessary until they are sitting straight. Leave to set, then mix a little epoxy and fill any gaps. It is easiest to use a cocktail stick to apply tiny amounts of the epoxy; if you should get any of the glue onto the shell, wait until it has almost set and then remove it with a sharp craft knife.

Paint the outer shell, spout and handle, and about 5mm (¼in) inside the base and lid. When the paint is dry, attach the teapot to the large filigree with some well-mixed epoxy.

Add the waterslide transfers, and then give the egg several coats of water-based varnish to seal in the transfers and give a nice glossy finish.

Line the egg using the circle method.

Attach a row of the fine gold cord around the cut edge of the base, followed by a row of the crystal chain, then more gold cord; finish with a row of the picot-edged braid. The lid has four rows of the fine gold cord with a row of the picot-edged braid to finish it off; cover the hinge with the braids as you go along.

Making sure they are central and look even from all angles, glue the filigrees to the top of the lid and finally glue a row of the crystal chain to the bottom of the egg where it sits in the base.

BELL

Bells make lovely Christmas gifts; or, instead of adding a filigree as I have done, you could use a wedding transfer to make an unusual wedding gift.

You will need the following:

- a tall, fat goose egg
- fine-grade glasspaper
- egg marker or elastic band
- hobby drill and 3mm (⅛in) drill bit
- paints, brush and/or sponge
- bell handle
- filigree
- fine gold cord
- gold looped cord
- wired ribbon
- epoxy resin and tacky glue.

Prepare the egg in the usual way. Mark in the cut line about ⅓ of the way from the pointed end of the egg, and cut the end away (Fig 11.2).

Clean the inside of the egg and fill the blowhole; when dry, rub down to a flush finish.

Paint the outer shell, and about 5mm (¼in) inside.

Attach a row of the gold cord around the cut edge of the egg, followed by a row of the crystal and pearl chain, then more gold cord and finally a row of the looped gold braid. Carefully bend the filigree so it will fit to the egg surface, and glue into position.

Using well-mixed epoxy, glue the handle to the top of the egg, sighting all round to make sure it is straight.

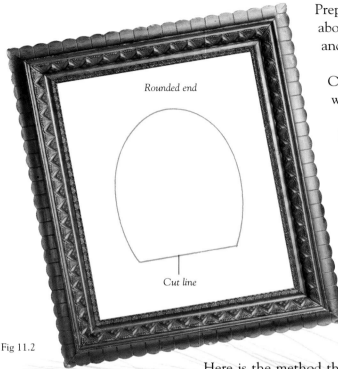

Rounded end

Cut line

Fig 11.2

Here is the method that I have used to line the blue egg. Make a small platform to go into the top of the egg. Pleat enough of the wired ribbon to fit the inside of the egg, stick Micropore to one edge and then trim away the wire, keeping a straight edge. Next, trim away the wire from the other edge. Apply glue to the inside of the egg and, with the tape towards the cut edge of the egg (in contact with the inside of the shell), press into position. Secure the folded edges with a row of the looped gold braid.

Cover the small platform with the pleated ribbon, and place a row of the looped gold braid at the outer edge, glued into the egg.

If you want to put a musical button inside the egg, leave out the platform. Make up the circular lining as before, glue the button into position at the top of the egg, then add the lining, finishing off with a row of the looped gold braid.

BABY CARRIAGE

The carriage lends itself beautifully to a Christening celebration or a first birthday. Change the colour to suit a boy or a girl.

You will need the following:

- a tall, fat goose egg
- fine-grade glasspaper
- egg marker or elastic band
- hobby drill and 3mm (⅛in) drill bit
- paints, brush and/or sponge
- baby carriage chassis
- ribbon, 5mm (¼in) wide
- small baby
- ultrafine polyflakes
- material to line the egg
- fine gold cord
- gold looped cord
- epoxy resin and tacky glue.

Prepare the egg in the usual way. Place into the egg marker and mark in six vertical lines over what will be the top half of the shell. Then, working from the fat end of the shell, mark in four girth lines about 5mm (¼in) apart. Remove the egg from the marker and then mark in the scalloped outline for the hood of the carriage (Fig 11.3). Next, using a tape measure and working from the centre near the hood, mark in the cut lines for the ribbon at regular intervals (Fig 11.4).

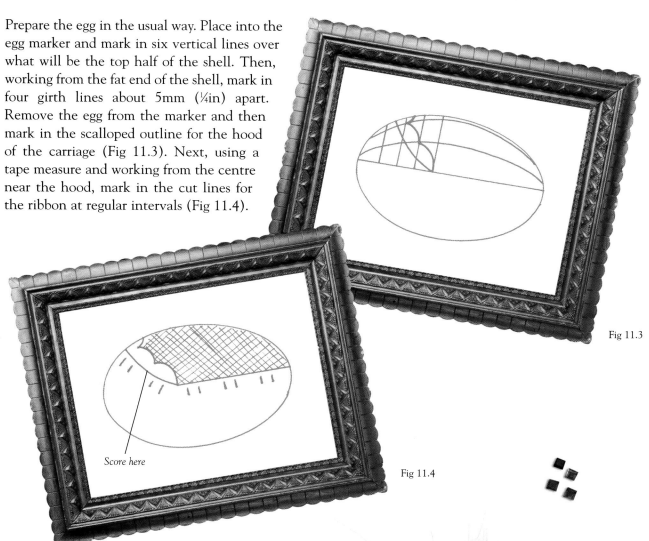

Fig 11.3

Score here

Fig 11.4

Score the guideline for the hood, cut the openings for the ribbon with the 3mm drill bit and then cut away the excess shell. Clean the inside of the shell and fill the blowhole; when dry, rub down to a smooth finish.

Paint the outer shell, being careful not to block the ribbon slits, and paint the inside of the hood and about 5mm (¼in) inside the shell.

Apply water-based varnish and ultrafine polyflakes to the outer edge of the hood and to the inside of the hood also.

Thread the ribbon through the slits in the shell and glue into position.

Make an oval lining, using the same technique as for a circular one, and glue into position; do not line the inside of the hood. Apply a row of the looped gold braid to the gathered edge of the lining.

Glue a row of the fine gold cord around the cut edge of the carriage all the way around and across the hood.

Paint the chassis if required, and glue the egg into position, making sure it is straight and even all of the way around.

Place the baby into the carriage.

CRIB

This is another ideal Christening present. For an alternative look, substitute lace for the wired ribbon, especially if the baby is a girl.

You will need the following:

- a tall, fat goose egg
- fine-grade glasspaper
- egg marker or elastic band
- hobby drill and 3mm (⅛in) drill bit
- paints, brush and/or sponge
- a stand suitable for use with a crib
- wired ribbon
- crystal and pearl chain
- small baby
- ultrafine polyflakes
- material to line the egg
- fine gold cord
- gold looped cord
- epoxy resin and tacky glue.

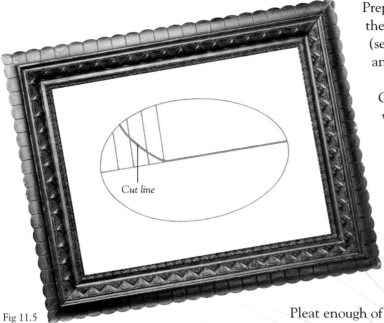

Fig 11.5

Cut line

Prepare the egg in the usual way, and mark in the same way as given for the Baby Carriage (see Fig 11.3). Remove from the egg marker and mark in for the hood (Fig 11.5).

Cut and clean the egg, fill the blowhole and, when dry, rub down to a smooth finish.

Paint the outer shell and about 5mm (¼in) inside.

Make an oval lining as for the Baby Carriage, and line the whole of the inside of the egg including the hood; add a row of the looped gold braid to the gathered edge.

Pleat enough of the wired ribbon to fit around the whole of the base of the egg. Secure one edge with the Micropore and cut away the wire as before, but do not cut the wire from what will be the lower edge; put to one side.

Pleat another small section of the ribbon to cover the hood; you may have to put this on in three sections as I did, depending on the width of the egg. Trim it to fit the hood shape. Secure both edges of the ribbon with Micropore and trim away the wire. Apply a thin coat of tacky glue to the hood and press the ribbon into place, with the pleats going across the hood; secure the centre section first and then the two outer sections.

Apply a thin coat of tacky glue all of the way around the edge of the base and, starting from the back near the hood, glue the skirt into position. Add looped gold braid to all of the cut edges, then add a row of the pearl and crystal chain to the top cut edge of the crib.

Glue the crib to the stand and place the baby inside.

TRICKS OF THE TRADE

- Always wear a face mask when rubbing down and cutting the eggshell, because prolonged exposure to the dust from the eggs can be hazardous.

- For textured finishes inside diorama-style eggs (eggs with a scene inside), a cheaper alternative to commercial products such as Ruff Stuff and No-Fire Snow is to mix some cornflour with water to a thick consistency, coat the inside of the egg and when dry paint to the desired finish. A couple of coats of Diamond Shimmer will add sparkle to snow scenes.

- Small mirrors are ideal for use as little ponds inside diorama eggs. Attach the mirror to the platform inside the egg and seal the edges and the rest of the platform with the cornflour mixture, leave to dry and then paint.

- To give a good enamelled effect to the shell, first draw in the design you want to enamel (for best results keep the sections small), then score in each section. Once the egg has been painted, outline the small sections with fine cord, making sure there are no gaps, and then paint in with enamel or glass paints. Alternatively, you could fill small sections at a time with epoxy resin mixed with a sprinkling of ultrafine polyflakes. It is important that you do a small section at a time and don't try to do two adjoining sections together.

- To enamel filigrees, first bend the filigree to fit the shape of the egg, then drizzle small amounts of epoxy resin onto the back of the filigree. Take your time and build up the coats of epoxy slowly. When the glue has set, paint the back in your chosen colours.

- To attach flat-back crystals and pearls to the shell, use a cocktail stick with a small amount of tacky glue on the tip; you just need to touch the crystal and it will pick up easily.

- To clean tacky glue from flat-backs and crystal chain, use a small amount of white vinegar on a cotton bud; this will not only remove the glue but it will also give the stones a lovely sparkle.

- Before cutting the lining for an egg, first outline the cutting line with tacky glue. This will make the cutting line easier to see and help to prevent the material from fraying at the cut edge.

- When fitting a full circular lining to the inside of the egg, try using a pair of curved tweezers to help manoeuvre the material inside the egg.

- Small pieces of broken eggshell give a good crazy-paving effect inside diorama-style eggs.

- If you find that your hinge has not gone on straight, don't despair: heat the hinge with a hairdryer, and as the glue warms it will soften enough for you to remove it carefully with a sharp craft knife.

- Try painting your filigrees and stands for a more dramatic effect. Coat the area to be painted with white acrylic gesso (this will give the final paint something to adhere to) and then, when the gesso has dried, paint with your chosen colours. A good flesh colour is 4 parts white, 1 part yellow and 1 part red.

I hope that you will get as much enjoyment from making these eggs as I did. As you become more accomplished, why not try taking different elements from different eggs to make up your own designs?

A useful way to gain experience (and spread the cost of the more expensive tools) is to join an 'egging circle'. If you don't have one in your area, why not start one up with a group of your friends?

Other crafts lend themselves well to egging, such as glass painting, stencilling, and using polymer clay to decorate the outer shell. Experiment and enjoy.

Though you may be able to find some of the necessary tools and equipment at your local craft shop, it is worth tracking down specialist eggcraft suppliers also. Many of these publish useful catalogues and instruction leaflets. I know of only a handful of suppliers in Britain; there are many more in the USA and Australia, who advertise on the Internet and in craft magazines.

ABOUT THE AUTHOR

Denise Hopper has always been interested in arts and craft subjects, and has become proficient at a number of different craft techniques, although she has had no formal training and has never been to art school. She is, for the most part, self-taught, using some of the many books available on the market today. She firmly believes that anyone can make these eggs, and that, with a little practice, a lot of patience and some imagination, anything is possible.

Denise is a single mother of four, and has lived in London with her sons since 1990.

INDEX OF

PROJECTS

* Items marked with an asterisk are suitable for making with a craft knife.

135

TITLES AVAILABLE FROM
GMC Publications
BOOKS

CRAFTS

American Patchwork Designs in Needlepoint	Melanie Tacon
Beginning Picture Marquetry	Lawrence Threadgold
Blackwork: A New Approach	Brenda Day
Celtic Cross Stitch Designs	Carol Phillipson
Celtic Knotwork Designs	Sheila Sturrock
Celtic Knotwork Handbook	Sheila Sturrock
Celtic Spirals and Other Designs	Sheila Sturrock
Complete Pyrography	Stephen Poole
Creative Backstitch	Helen Hall
Creative Embroidery Techniques Using Colour Through Gold	
	Daphne J. Ashby & Jackie Woolsey
The Creative Quilter: Techniques and Projects	Pauline Brown
Cross-Stitch Designs from China	Carol Phillipson
Decoration on Fabric: A Sourcebook of Ideas	Pauline Brown
Decorative Beaded Purses	Enid Taylor
Designing and Making Cards	Glennis Gilruth
Glass Engraving Pattern Book	John Everett
Glass Painting	Emma Sedman
Handcrafted Rugs	Sandra Hardy
How to Arrange Flowers: A Japanese Approach to English Design	
	Taeko Marvelly
How to Make First-Class Cards	Debbie Brown
An Introduction to Crewel Embroidery	Mave Glenny
Making and Using Working Drawings for Realistic Model Animals	
	Basil F. Fordham
Making Character Bears	Valerie Tyler
Making Decorative Screens	Amanda Howes
Making Fabergé-Style Eggs	Denise Hopper
Making Fairies and Fantastical Creatures	Julie Sharp
Making Greetings Cards for Beginners	Pat Sutherland
Making Hand-Sewn Boxes: Techniques and Projects	Jackie Woolsey
Making Knitwear Fit	Pat Ashforth & Steve Plummer
Making Mini Cards, Gift Tags & Invitations	Glennis Gilruth
Making Soft-Bodied Dough Characters	Patricia Hughes
Natural Ideas for Christmas: Fantastic Decorations to Make	
	Josie Cameron-Ashcroft & Carol Cox
New Ideas for Crochet: Stylish Projects for the Home	Darsha Capaldi
Papercraft Projects for Special Occasions	Sine Chesterman
Patchwork for Beginners	Pauline Brown
Pyrography Designs	Norma Gregory
Pyrography Handbook (Practical Crafts)	Stephen Poole
Rose Windows for Quilters	Angela Besley
Rubber Stamping with Other Crafts	Lynne Garner
Sponge Painting	Ann Rooney
Stained Glass: Techniques and Projects	Mary Shanahan
Step-by-Step Pyrography Projects for the Solid Point Machine	
	Norma Gregory
Tassel Making for Beginners	Enid Taylor
Tatting Collage	Lindsay Rogers
Tatting Patterns	Lyn Morton
Temari: A Traditional Japanese Embroidery Technique	Margaret Ludlow
Trip Around the World: 25 Patchwork, Quilting and Appliqué Projects	
	Gail Lawther
Trompe l'Oeil: Techniques and Projects	Jan Lee Johnson
Tudor Treasures to Embroider	Pamela Warner
Wax Art	Hazel Marsh

DOLLS' HOUSES AND MINIATURES

1/12 Scale Character Figures for the Dolls' House	James Carrington
Americana in 1/12 Scale: 50 Authentic Projects	
	Joanne Ogreenc & Mary Lou Santovec
Architecture for Dolls' Houses	Joyce Percival
The Authentic Georgian Dolls' House	Brian Long
A Beginners' Guide to the Dolls' House Hobby	Jean Nisbett
Celtic, Medieval and Tudor Wall Hangings in 1/12 Scale Needlepoint	
	Sandra Whitehead
Creating Decorative Fabrics: Projects in 1/12 Scale	Janet Storey
The Dolls' House 1/24 Scale: A Complete Introduction	Jean Nisbett
Dolls' House Accessories, Fixtures and Fittings	Andrea Barham
Dolls' House Furniture: Easy-to-Make Projects in 1/12 Scale	Freida Gray
Dolls' House Makeovers	Jean Nisbett
Dolls' House Window Treatments	Eve Harwood
Easy to Make Dolls' House Accessories	Andrea Barham
Edwardian-Style Hand-Knitted Fashion for 1/12 Scale Dolls	
	Yvonne Wakefield
How to Make Your Dolls' House Special: Fresh Ideas for Decorating	
	Beryl Armstrong
Make Your Own Dolls' House Furniture	Maurice Harper
Making Dolls' House Furniture	Patricia King
Making Georgian Dolls' Houses	Derek Rowbottom
Making Miniature Chinese Rugs and Carpets	Carol Phillipson
Making Miniature Food and Market Stalls	Angie Scarr
Making Miniature Gardens	Freida Gray
Making Miniature Oriental Rugs & Carpets	Meik & Ian McNaughton
Making Period Dolls' House Accessories	Andrea Barham
Making Tudor Dolls' Houses	Derek Rowbottom
Making Victorian Dolls' House Furniture	Patricia King
Miniature Bobbin Lace	Roz Snowden
Miniature Embroidery for the Georgian Dolls' House	Pamela Warner
Miniature Embroidery for the Tudor and Stuart Dolls' House	
	Pamela Warner
Miniature Embroidery for the Victorian Dolls' House	Pamela Warner
Miniature Needlepoint Carpets	Janet Granger
More Miniature Oriental Rugs & Carpets	Meik & Ian McNaughton
Needlepoint 1/12 Scale: Design Collections for the Dolls' House	
	Felicity Price
New Ideas for Miniature Bobbin Lace	Roz Snowden
The Secrets of the Dolls' House Makers	Jean Nisbett

UPHOLSTERY

The Upholsterer's Pocket Reference Book	David James
Upholstery: A Complete Course (Revised Edition)	David James
Upholstery Restoration	David James
Upholstery Techniques & Projects	David James
Upholstery Tips and Hints	David James

TOYMAKING

Scrollsaw Toy Projects — *Ivor Carlyle*
Scrollsaw Toys for All Ages — *Ivor Carlyle*

GARDENING

Auriculas for Everyone: How to Grow and Show Perfect Plants — *Mary Robinson*
Beginners' Guide to Herb Gardening — *Yvonne Cuthbertson*
Beginners' Guide to Water Gardening — *Graham Clarke*
Bird Boxes and Feeders for the Garden — *Dave Mackenzie*
The Birdwatcher's Garden — *Hazel & Pamela Johnson*
Broad-Leaved Evergreens — *Stephen G. Haw*
Companions to Clematis: Growing Clematis with Other Plants — *Marigold Badcock*
Creating Contrast with Dark Plants — *Freya Martin*
Creating Small Habitats for Wildlife in your Garden — *Josie Briggs*
Exotics are Easy — *GMC Publications*
Gardening with Hebes — *Chris & Valerie Wheeler*
Gardening with Wild Plants — *Julian Slatcher*
Growing Cacti and Other Succulents in the Conservatory and Indoors — *Shirley-Anne Bell*
Growing Cacti and Other Succulents in the Garden — *Shirley-Anne Bell*
Hardy Perennials: A Beginner's Guide — *Eric Sawford*
Hedges: Creating Screens and Edges — *Averil Bedrich*
The Living Tropical Greenhouse: Creating a Haven for Butterflies — *John & Maureen Tampion*
Marginal Plants — *Bernard Sleeman*
Orchids are Easy: A Beginner's Guide to their Care and Cultivation — *Tom Gilland*
Plant Alert: A Garden Guide for Parents — *Catherine Collins*
Planting Plans for Your Garden — *Jenny Shukman*
Plants that Span the Seasons — *Roger Wilson*
Sink and Container Gardening Using Dwarf Hardy Plants — *Chris & Valerie Wheeler*
The Successful Conservatory and Growing Exotic Plants — *Joan Phelan*
Tropical Garden Style with Hardy Plants — *Alan Hemsley*
Water Garden Projects: From Groundwork to Planting — *Roger Sweetinburgh*

WOODCARVING

Beginning Woodcarving — *GMC Publications*
Carving Architectural Detail in Wood: The Classical Tradition — *Frederick Wilbur*
Carving Birds & Beasts — *GMC Publications*
Carving the Human Figure: Studies in Wood and Stone — *Dick Onians*
Carving Nature: Wildlife Studies in Wood — *Frank Fox-Wilson*
Carving on Turning — *Chris Pye*
Decorative Woodcarving — *Jeremy Williams*
Elements of Woodcarving — *Chris Pye*
Essential Woodcarving Techniques — *Dick Onians*
Lettercarving in Wood: A Practical Course — *Chris Pye*
Making & Using Working Drawings for Realistic Model Animals — *Basil F. Fordham*
Power Tools for Woodcarving — *David Tippey*
Relief Carving in Wood: A Practical Introduction — *Chris Pye*
Understanding Woodcarving in the Round — *GMC Publications*
Useful Techniques for Woodcarvers — *GMC Publications*
Woodcarving: A Foundation Course — *Zoë Gertner*
Woodcarving for Beginners — *GMC Publications*
Woodcarving Tools, Materials & Equipment (New Edition in 2 vols.) — *Chris Pye*

WOODTURNING

Adventures in Woodturning — *David Springett*
Bowl Turning Techniques Masterclass — *Tony Boase*
Chris Child's Projects for Woodturners — *Chris Child*
Colouring Techniques for Woodturners — *Jan Sanders*
Contemporary Turned Wood: New Perspectives in a Rich Tradition — *Ray Leier, Jan Peters & Kevin Wallace*
The Craftsman Woodturner — *Peter Child*
Decorating Turned Wood: The Maker's Eye — *Liz & Michael O'Donnell*
Decorative Techniques for Woodturners — *Hilary Bowen*
Illustrated Woodturning Techniques — *John Hunnex*
Intermediate Woodturning Projects — *GMC Publications*
Keith Rowley's Woodturning Projects — *Keith Rowley*
Making Screw Threads in Wood — *Fred Holder*
Turned Boxes: 50 Designs — *Chris Stott*
Turning Green Wood — *Michael O'Donnell*
Turning Pens and Pencils — *Kip Christensen & Rex Burningham*
Useful Woodturning Projects — *GMC Publications*
Woodturning: Bowls, Platters, Hollow Forms, Vases, Vessels, Bottles, Flasks, Tankards, Plates — *GMC Publications*
Woodturning: A Foundation Course (New Edition) — *Keith Rowley*
Woodturning: A Fresh Approach — *Robert Chapman*
Woodturning: An Individual Approach — *Dave Regester*
Woodturning: A Source Book of Shapes — *John Hunnex*
Woodturning Jewellery — *Hilary Bowen*
Woodturning Masterclass — *Tony Boase*
Woodturning Techniques — *GMC Publications*

WOODWORKING

Advanced Scrollsaw Projects — *GMC Publications*
Beginning Picture Marquetry — *Lawrence Threadgold*
Bird Boxes and Feeders for the Garden — *Dave Mackenzie*
Celtic Carved Lovespoons: 30 Patterns — *Sharon Littley & Clive Griffin*
Celtic Woodcraft — *Glenda Bennett*
Complete Woodfinishing — *Ian Hosker*
David Charlesworth's Furniture-Making Techniques — *David Charlesworth*
David Charlesworth's Furniture-Making Techniques – Volume 2 — *David Charlesworth*
The Encyclopedia of Joint Making — *Terrie Noll*
Furniture-Making Projects for the Wood Craftsman — *GMC Publications*
Furniture-Making Techniques for the Wood Craftsman — *GMC Publications*
Furniture Restoration (Practical Crafts) — *Kevin Jan Bonner*
Furniture Restoration: A Professional at Work — *John Lloyd*
Furniture Restoration and Repair for Beginners — *Kevin Jan Bonner*
Furniture Restoration Workshop — *Kevin Jan Bonner*
Green Woodwork — *Mike Abbott*
Intarsia: 30 Patterns for the Scrollsaw — *John Everett*
Kevin Ley's Furniture Projects — *Kevin Ley*
Making Chairs and Tables — *GMC Publications*
Making Chairs and Tables – Volume 2 — *GMC Publications*
Making Classic English Furniture — *Paul Richardson*
Making Heirloom Boxes — *Peter Lloyd*
Making Little Boxes from Wood — *John Bennett*
Making Screw Threads in Wood — *Fred Holder*
Making Shaker Furniture — *Barry Jackson*
Making Woodwork Aids and Devices — *Robert Wearing*
Mastering the Router — *Ron Fox*
Pine Furniture Projects for the Home — *Dave Mackenzie*
Practical Scrollsaw Patterns — *John Everett*
Router Magic: Jigs, Fixtures and Tricks to Unleash your Router's Full Potential — *Bill Hylton*

PHOTOGRAPHY

ART TECHNIQUES

VIDEOS

MAGAZINES

WOODTURNING ◆ WOODCARVING ◆ FURNITURE & CABINETMAKING
THE ROUTER ◆ NEW WOODWORKING ◆ THE DOLLS' HOUSE MAGAZINE
OUTDOOR PHOTOGRAPHY ◆ BLACK & WHITE PHOTOGRAPHY
MACHINE KNITTING NEWS ◆ BUSINESSMATTERS

The above represents a full list of all titles currently published or scheduled to be published.
All are available direct from the Publishers or through bookshops, newsagents and specialist retailers.
To place an order, or to obtain a complete catalogue, contact:

GMC Publications,
Castle Place, 166 High Street, Lewes, East Sussex BN7 1XU, United Kingdom
Tel: 01273 488005 Fax: 01273 478606
E-mail: pubs@thegmcgroup.com

Orders by credit card are accepted